About KidLit-O

KidLit-O is an imprint of BookCaps™ that is just for kids! Each month BookCaps will be releasing several books in this exciting imprint. Visit are website or like us on Facebook to see more!

To add your name to our mailing list, visit this link:
http://www.kidlito.com/mailing-list.html

Leonardo Da Vinci

Introduction

If you take a trip to the museum, you will see plenty of art: pictures, paintings, sculptures, murals, and so on. For literally thousands of years, human beings have been creating art using whatever materials they can. From using the juice of berries to painting images on the walls of caves to using chisels to create a man of stone, art is a hugely vital part of society.

But what is art used for? Well, many people use it to express *ideas*. Just like books and songs, each piece of artwork contains a message. People love to talk about art, and the way that it makes them feel; the greatest works of art will make different people feel different things.

When you are studying art, there is one famous person that you cannot miss. His name was Leonardo da Vinci, and even hundreds of years after his death, his name has not faded. Perhaps you have heard of the *Mona Lisa*, one of his most famous works. Da Vinci was a genius in his time, and even in our modern era, millions of people marvel at his excellent work. Leonardo da Vinci is not only famous for his paintings, but he was also a scientist and an inventor. Many of his ideas we use today. As we look back on his drawings and sketches, we can see how brilliant and advanced his mind was.

But who *was* da Vinci? Why was he so famous? At a single glance, the *Mona Lisa* just looks like a normal painting of a woman. Why is his artwork celebrated around the globe, and for hundreds of years? Da Vinci's life was intriguing. In order to understand his art and the impact it had on people, we must first understand his life.

Chapter 1: Early Childhood

Leonardo da Vinci was born hundreds of years ago – over *five hundred years ago*, in fact. On April 15th of 1452, approximately forty years before Christopher Columbus explored the Americas, Leonardo da Vinci was born in Italy. In Italian, the word "da" means "of," and "Vinci" is the small in which Leonardo was born. This was how many people were identified during this time period; he was known as Leonardo who came from the town Vinci (pronounced *vin-chee*).

Historians know that Leonardo's mother's name was Caterina (the Italian form of *Catherine*), but no one knows what her last name was, or what she used as a last name. Caterina was young, and she had barely any money. She was a *peasant*, which means she was poor. Today, we say that people are low class (poor), middle class (okay), or high class (rich). Caterina was a member of the low class, and she could not afford to take care of her child.

As if Caterina's money troubles weren't enough, Leonardo's father was terrible. His name was Ser Piero, and he had much more money than Caterina. However, he never wanted to marry her. When Leonardo was born, Ser Piero was disgusted. He did not want to be tied down with a peasant mother and a son who would remain in the low class. Ser Piero left Caterina and Leonardo so that he could marry another woman. He found someone who was not in the lower class, and he had other children that he actually wanted to take care of. Meanwhile, Caterina was left with a child that she could not afford to have.

Caterina wanted a husband, though. She cared for Leonardo, but after her child had grown to be two years old, she decided that she needed to give Leonardo away. But to whom? Caterina contacted Ser Piero and asked him what they should do with the child. Ser Piero, who did not want to discuss Leonardo at all, told Caterina to give the child to his grandparents. Ser Piero's mother and father were almost too old to care for children anymore. Would sending Leonardo to live with them truly be the right choice?

Catherina took the opportunity. Leonardo's grandparents took him into their home and decided to take care of him. However, like Caterina and Ser Piero, they weren't the best caretakers. Of course, they gave him food and shelter, but beyond that they did nothing. Leonardo needed *someone* to look up to, to have some sort of role model in his life. Who would he have, if his grandparents, Caterina, and Ser Piero would not help him?

That is where Leonardo's uncle came into his life. His uncle's name was Francesco, and he was a positive role model in Leonardo's life. Francesco was a farmer; at the time, many of the low class peasants were farmers. Together, Francesco and Leonardo went on walks around the Italian countryside. If you have never been to Italy, you should know that the landscapes there are beautiful.

Leonardo grew up with rolling hills of green grass and sloping mountains peppered with trees, jutting into blue skies with fluffy white clouds. Italy is known for its abundant olive trees and its gorgeous vineyards. If you want to understand how Leonardo became such a genius, it is important to understand what he did as a child.

When he and Francesco would go for walks, Leonardo would often draw the things that he saw. It started with some practice and some imagination. He sketched everything from a flower on the ground to the birds flying overhead, from the horizon to the glaring sun. Continuing to practice made Leonardo an excellent artist, although many people say that he was born with the talent. Nevertheless, constantly drawing made Leonardo better. Practice makes perfect!

People around the town began to notice and hear about the blooming young artist. While many young people were skilled at drawing at the time, Leonardo's imaginative and vivid works took people's breath away. His father Ser Piero heard that Leonardo had talent, and he took interest in his son. Ser Piero knew that because Leonardo was poor, he would never be able to get a proper education and go anywhere in life. But after some careful consideration, Ser Piero contacted his son. He told Leonardo that he was to become an apprentice to a famous artist.

When someone becomes an apprentice, they assist an experienced person. It is a fantastic opportunity to learn more about a certain subject and get more knowledge. Today, we do not typically use the word "apprentice," but instead use the word "intern." An *intern* is someone that works at a job, sometimes for no pay, to gain experience. Even though Leonardo was extremely talented for his age, having an apprenticeship can pay off in the end. He knew that he was on the road to fame, and the apprenticeship would help him.

Chapter 2: Learning to Be a Professional Artist

Ser Piero sent Leonardo to the Italian city of Florence. If you have not heard of it, Florence is one of Italy's most famous cities. It is known for its artwork and tourist attractions, such as museums and old churches. In Leonardo da Vinci's time, Florence was popular because it was a center for talented artists.

Leonardo's new master was named Andrea del Verrocchio, and he lived in Florence. He was a hugely famous artist, and he lived in the perfect city for the job. Leonardo was happy to go to Florence. If he wanted to become a famous artist, spending some time in Florence was necessary. Verrocchio did not pay Leonardo for the work that he did; however, he did provide Leonardo with food and a roof over his head. On top of that, the experience that Leonardo gained was invaluable.

Leonardo lived with many other boys, who were also apprentices of Verrochio. Verrochio taught them many important things to artists: how to work with different materials, how to paint onto walls, how to sculpt statues, and more. But making art was not the only thing Leonardo had to do. He also had to *make* the paint and the paintbrushes. But how could Leonardo make his own materials?

Well, back then, the bristles of a paintbrush was made out of animal hair. Leonardo needed the hair of animals such as hogs and squirrels. They would attach the hair to small wooden sticks and have their very own paintbrushes. But what about the paint? Today, paint is mainly made out of colored oil. But hundreds of years ago, different colors were made with hugely different materials.

If Leonardo needed to paint with red, he needed to find beetles and crush them. This would create a red color. Some of the other colors came from grinding stones, and others came from crushing berries. This may sound weird now because anyone can go into the store and purchase a set of paint. But Verrocchio taught Leonardo how to make his own paint.

So, what exactly did Leonardo make while he stayed in Verrocchio's art studio? Customers would come to Verrocchio and ask for certain paintings: sometimes it would be a portrait, sometimes a drawing of a beautiful landscape. Verrocchio took all of the orders and assigned them to his many apprentices. Despite being a supremely talented artist, Verrocchio rarely did any of the work. He taught his apprentices, of course, but he mainly dealt with the business side of everything.

Think of Verrocchio's art studio as a ladder. Each apprentice enters the studio on the bottom rung of the ladder—the very bottom step. This bottom step includes running errands for Verrocchio, cleaning the studio, and other small tasks. After a while, the apprentices are allowed to climb up to the next step and go higher. The hugely talented apprentices rise even higher on the ladder and can paint advanced projects.

Even though Leonardo started on the bottom rung of the ladder, he quickly rose to the top. Verrocchio could see how skilled he was at interpreting life and throwing it onto a painting. Verrocchio soon realized that Leonardo was better than him. Leonardo knew how to bring people to life using a paintbrush. He knew how to create gorgeous and realistic landscapes that could make people stare at them in wonder. People began to realize that Leonardo's work surpassed his master's by far.

After thirteen years at Verrocchio's art studio, Leonardo finally decided it was time to leave. By this time, he was a master himself, and more talented than ever. People around Florence and Italy started to hear his name everywhere and talk about his work. After he left Verrocchio's studio, Leonardo wanted to learn more than just artwork. He had never attended a university before since he was too poor as a child and had spent the rest of his years working for Verrocchio.

Around this time, books were becoming more popular. Today, we are darned lucky to have bookshops around every corner and books in plenty of stores. But in Leonardo's time, books were not automatically printed with ink. Instead, someone with extremely neat handwriting to write down each book by hand—a task that could take months to accomplish. And if this person made one error, they had to start over. But Leonardo was lucky enough to live during a time in which the printing press was invented.

The *printing press* is one of the most revolutionary inventions in all of human history. Books could now be printed and copied by a machine exceptionally easily, and this meant that more books could reach the public. More people began to read, and one of these people was Leonardo da Vinci. He wanted to learn more and more about the world around him, so he started a massive collection of educational books.

He continued to paint and learn throughout his twenties, but when he turned thirty, Leonardo realized that the once-prosperous city of Florence was no longer so great. The two most powerful families in the city were at war with each other, similar to the two warring families in *Romeo and Juliet* by William Shakespeare, perhaps the greatest storyteller to ever live. Leonardo wanted to move away from all the danger, so he traveled northward to the Italian city of Milan.

It is a commonly known fact that Leonardo da Vinci was *ambidextrous*, which means he was neither left nor right-handed. He could write with both hands! Because of this, he would often write from right to left on a piece of paper, and he would even write the letters backwards. A person could only read them if the paper was held up to a mirror! Some people say that Leonardo's friends and family could not decipher any of his notes because they could not understand what all the strange symbols were. Some theories say that Leonardo wrote this way to stop people from reading his ideas and stealing them. Other people say that Leonardo was just a bit odd, and he liked to have some fun when he wrote down his ideas.

Chapter 3: Professional Works

Even though Milan was not as famous as Florence, Leonardo still knew that he would do well there. He was interested in working for the duke of Milan—a *duke* is someone who rules over a large area of land. Back then, a *duke* would be like a *governor* today. The duke's name was Ludovico Sforza, and he was in need of many things. Sforza hired Leonardo to work for him, to create paintings, instruments, and even a theatre stage. Leonardo was not just good at painting—he was a master builder too!

One of da Vinci's most intriguing works was built for the duke of Milan. The duke wanted Leonardo to build a horse—but not just a simple life-size horse. He wanted an enormous statue, in memory of his father.

Leonardo knew that this would be no easy task. This sculpture of a horse would need to be *perfect*, especially if the duke wanted it to be so large. Leonardo studied horses both alive and dead. He went into the stables and examined the way that the horses stood and moved. He looked inside dead horses so that he could see their organs and their muscle structure. Only once he knew *everything* about horses could he create the perfect sculpture.

In total, it took Leonardo da Vinci ten whole years to finish his sculpture of the horse. He needed eighty tons of metal (160,000 pounds), which was unprecedented. It stood twenty-four feet tall, and it looked magnificent as it stood in a prancing style in front of Duke Sforza's castle.

So, why was it so momentous? Sure, people loved looking at the horse because it was enormous. It was a spectacle for people around Italy to come and look at. But it was so significant because of all the time that Leonardo da Vinci took with it. He needed each hair on the horse's mane and tail to be perfect. The movement of the horse needed to look exactly like how a normal horse would move. It was supposed to be the largest sculpture ever casted in bronze.

The horse was made out of clay, and Leonardo had planned to cover it with bronze. This would make it look much more official. But Leonardo was never given the bronze that he needed because Duke Sforza used it to make cannons. At the time that Leonardo da Vinci was there, the armies of France were invading Milan.

Unfortunately, the city of Milan was unable to defend itself against the powerful forces of the French armies. The French successfully invaded the city—and Leonardo's famous horse statue did not survive the occupation. When the French soldiers found the horse, they did not marvel at it like everyone else. Instead, they used it for archery practice. *Archery* is the use of bows and arrows.

While Leonardo had been working on the horse, he had an apprentice with him. Leonardo often thought about all of the time that he spent as an apprentice when he was a kid. Starting as a poor boy doing chores, Leonardo had grown to become one of the most famous artists on the planet. Leonardo was excited to have an apprentice of his own: a young boy who was called Giacomo.

Giacomo did not have a family and had spent much of his childhood alone. Leonardo took the boy under his roof so he could have shelter, food, a terrific role model, and education. Little did Leonardo know that the boy Giacomo would become one of his greatest friends. Leonardo liked to call Giacomo "Salai," which stands for "scoundrel." This was because Giacomo was generally a misbehaved child. He did not hesitate to steal from Leonardo, pull pranks, and eat more than his share of food.

Most masters would have thrown Salai out immediately—but not Leonardo. Despite the fact that Salai was mischievous, Leonardo liked him. The two of them traveled everywhere together, and they became lifelong friends. Some people even believe that Salai is actually the person in the *Mona Lisa* painting—but we will talk more about the *Mona Lisa* later.

But before the French even invaded Milan, Leonardo da Vinci had another project on his hands. His next project was not a sculpture, but a painting: a painting that would go down in history as one of the most famous works of art. Duke Sforza told Leonardo that he wanted a painting for the monastery in which he would one day be buried. Leonardo thought long and hard about what the painting would be about, and he finally came up with an idea.

To this day, the religion of *Christianity* is one of the world's most popular religions. Christians believe in one God, and the teachings of Jesus Christ. According to Christians, Jesus is the *messiah*, the savior of the world's people. Christians believe that Jesus performed many miracles in the name of God, including feeding the poor, walking on water, and coming back to life. They also believe that Jesus sacrificed his life so that the sins of humanity would be forgiven.

Leonardo da Vinci was a Christian. He thought about what scenes from Jesus's life he could paint and bring to life, and he decided on the "last supper." According to the Bible, the night before Jesus died, he brought together his twelve disciples (*disciples* means *followers*) and ate dinner with them. This is referred to as the "last supper."

This would be a creative and unique scene to paint—but to make things even more difficult for Leonardo, he would not be using a canvas. He wanted to paint on the walls of the monastery dining room. When an artist paints on the walls, they are painting a *fresco. Frescos* are difficult because the paint cannot be erased, and it dries very quickly. Leonardo would need all of his skills and all of his talent if he wished to successfully paint this image of Jesus's last supper.

When Leonardo started work on the painting, it took up all of his time. Hours upon hours, days upon days, weeks upon weeks went into making sure the painting was the absolute best it could be. He decided he wished to call it *The Last Supper.* When people in Italy heard what Leonardo was painting, they couldn't wait to come and see it. Leonardo's talent was well known across the country, and plenty of people were Christian. Many Italians had only read the words of the Bible; it would have been an interesting sight to see the Bible come alive on a painting!

Leonardo worked day and night, sometimes refusing to eat or drink anything all day. He was intensely focused on his work. The eyes of all of Italy were on him to produce the most spectacular painting the world had ever seen. He finished *The Last Supper* in the year 1497, about two years before the French invaded Milan.

So, what is so important about this painting? Why is it still reproduced today as one of the most important paintings in history? At the time, many people had tried to depict Jesus's "last supper," but all of the attempts were complete failures. No one had the talent that Leonardo had. Leonardo was able to bring Jesus to life, along with all of the emotions of his twelve disciples. To many people, even today, the painting is incredibly realistic. To devout Christians, this is an excellent way to view the events in the Bible.

If you see a picture of *The Last Supper*, study it closely. Notice how Jesus Christ is in the very center of the painting, and how his disciples' hands all aim towards him. This is because Jesus is the Son of God. Everyone in the painting revolved around him, signifying that Jesus is incredibly important. Also notice that everyone in the painting is talking and seems to be in an uproar—besides Jesus, of course. Why is this?

Jesus told the disciples at the last supper that one of them would betray him—and one of them did. His name was Judas, and he was the reason that Jesus was sentenced to death. Judas can be seen in the painting. But Jesus is not concerned that there is a traitor in his midst because he knows that he come back to life and go to Heaven.

The wall on which *The Last Supper* was painted is still standing today, although the painting does not look so great. The paint started to peel a few decades after it was completed, and many people have tried to make it look better over the centuries. If you are searching for a clear picture of the painting, it might be better to search for a recreation of it.

For years, many people have thought that there are hidden messages hidden within the painting, perhaps secrets that can tell us about Jesus Christ. Many of the most popular ideas have appeared in the novel *The Da Vinci Code*. People will always speculate about *The Last Supper*, but it still proudly stands as a leftover of one of the world's most talented artists.

Part of the reason that Leonardo da Vinci's artwork was so momentous was because he did outline what he put on the canvas. Today, if we draw a picture, we might use a dark line to outline the image, and then color it in afterward. Leonardo did not do this. Instead, he just used dark and light colors and carefully put them onto the canvas in the shape of whatever he wanted. Not many artists had used this idea before, and barely any had been successful. Leonardo da Vinci was a pioneer for a new style of art, one that would change the world forever.

Chapter 4: Leonardo's Ideas and Designs

Leonardo had just enough time to finish the sculpture of the horse and the painting of *The Last Supper* before his life was thrown into danger. Milan was not a safe city once the armies of France attacked. Just like his time spent in Florence, Leonardo would now need to find a new place to live. And who better to go with him than his apprentice Salai!

Leonardo and Salai left Milan in the year 1499. They were not exactly sure they wanted to stay in one place. The world was big and wide, and there were plenty of excellent opportunities before them. In addition, many people wanted to know what Leonardo would do next. They wanted to see his paintings and his sculptures.

But when he wasn't busy with the paintbrush, Leonardo had other things on his mind. In fact, Leonardo was more than just a genius. He was a creative and logical thinker, and he wanted to invent new things. He was inspired by the world around him, which is why he kept a notebook with him at all times. He liked to draw the things that he saw, just like he did when he was only an apprentice with Verrochio.

Leonardo had dozens of notebooks, filled with all of his ideas and his drawings. Some of his pages included ideas that some people may have thought were crazy at the time. Leonardo thought of inventions that would allow humans to fly in the air, and even walk on water. While we still have not found ways to walk on water, Leonardo's ideas about flying were hugely important in the creation of the first airplane.

Orville and Wilbur Wright were two men that, in the early 1900s, wanted to create the first airplane. They were successful, but of course the drawings of Leonardo da Vinci helped. Leonardo had lived four hundred years earlier, which shows that ideas for airplane-like inventions were not new.

It is important to know that Leonardo da Vinci was not only a painter. Sure, he is best known for the *Mona Lisa* and *The Last Supper*, but we also have to understand that he was more than an artistic genius. He was creative, logical, and extremely intelligent, which makes him one of the greatest minds of his time. There is a reason that we still talk about him today!

Leonardo's drawings were phenomenal and innovative at the time. Some people say that he used over *ten thousand* pages to detail his drawings, ideas, and cool inventions. While not all of them have survived, the ones that do exist have sold for millions of dollars. Why? Because they are a priceless piece of history. To hold the exact pages that Leonardo da Vinci wrote on would be an incredible feeling. Leonardo's ideas were the start of much of our modern technology, and if we want to understand our current world, we will need to understand the past.

Let us say that you get the chance to read one of Leonardo's notebook pages. Upon seeing it, you would notice something very odd. It looks like Leonardo da Vinci wrote an alien language! Of course, he spoke and wrote in Italian, but Italian uses the same letters as English does. So why do his letters look so weird? Well, Leonardo is known for his strange writing, which was always written backwards.

In order for a person to easily read Leonardo's words, he or she would need to hold the paper up to a mirror and read it in the glass. Many historians and scholars have tried to figure out why Leonardo wrote this way, but no one has a clear answer. Some say it was because he was afraid that people would try to steal his ideas and that any thieves would immediately be confused by the strange appearance of his letters. Others think that it was easier for Leonardo to write this way because he was left-handed. Anyone who is left-handed knows that pencil lead and ink can sometimes smudge the side of your hand since your hand drags on whatever you just wrote on the left. So if Leonardo instead wrote from right-to-left, instead of left-to-write, his hand would not be smudged.

Either way, it is clear that Leonardo was an interesting man with an interesting brain. He never stopped thinking of ideas that would amaze people. In his travels, he eventually came to the city of Valentinois. There, he found more official work, and was more than happy to start painting and building again. The duke of the city, named Cesare Borgia, was known for being a cruel man. At this time, Italy was still warring with France, and Cesare Borgia was one of the most ruthless politicians at the time.

Cesare Borgia wanted Leonardo to work for him. Of course, he had heard how Leonardo had praised and worked for Duke Sforza in Milan, and Borgia wanted the same great service. Leonardo was happy to work for Borgia, although he did not care much for the war. He just wanted to work.

Borgia told Leonardo that he needed new weapons and ideas that would give Italy the upper hand in battle. Leonardo immediately set off to work. While he did not build any of his ideas, he had fun drawing them. Things like enormous bows the size of a human, that could fire a dozen arrows at once, and chariots with whirling blades in the front were just a couple of Leonardo's whacky ideas. Of course, they may well have worked, but they were unfortunately never put into practice. Leonardo did not care though. He did not like it when soldiers fought each other; he only worked for Cesare Borgia because he liked to design new things.

Chapter 5: Da Vinci and the Human Body

Leonardo's works are often loved for how well they show the human body. Before him, few artists could recreate human beings so perfectly. Leonardo da Vinci brought the world around him to life, especially the people that he saw. Many of his drawings of machines inspired his drawings of humans because he knew that humans worked in a machine-like way. We have arms that can swing and pivot and grab, our legs have a specific motion to them, and our bodies are perfectly constructed so that we can survive.

Leonardo was obviously not the first person to be fascinated with the human body, but he is partly so famous for his work with human *anatomy*—how humans are built. So, how exactly did Leonardo learn so much about humans? Well, he used dead bodies and studied them intensely. He would often cut them open using medical tools, and inspect the inside of the bodies. Leonardo knew that if he wanted to understand human beings, he needed to look at the *inside* as well as the *outside*. Today, we have plastic models and diagrams, but Leonardo needed to learn from experience. Many of the medical students during Leonardo's time did not perform dissections since this was considered unsafe and disgusting—so, instead, the students learned all of the necessary medical information from books. Leonardo knew that this was not a particularly good way to gain first-hand experience.

Technically, Leonardo was not a licensed doctor or even a medical student. Because of this, it was not legal for him to dissect bodies. But he wanted to learn so badly that he did it anyways. Many historians think that Leonardo da Vinci dissected as many as thirty human bodies in the dead of night—and that he had been doing this for years, since before he arrived in Milan. Leonardo did not enjoy it—the bodies smelled bad, and he did not like seeing the inside of a human being. But the results of his work were incredible, and we still marvel over his drawings today.

Leonardo da Vinci studied human muscles, human bones, and human organs, drawing them in the many different ways that they could move and function. He would draw hands on the paper, and outline all the various bones and muscles that moved beneath our skin. Leonardo was hugely ambitious, and he is partly famous for the work he did in human anatomy. Barely anyone at the time had dug so deep into the human body to study it, so Leonardo became even more famous for this. Scientists and doctors at the time were intrigued to see Leonardo's drawings.

Here is something that many people do not know: Leonardo da Vinci created the idea for the first robot. He thought that, since humans acted like machines, it might even be possible to build a living machine. He wanted to build a "robotic" human, made of metal, which was dressed in a knight's armor. While Leonardo clearly never built his robot, his ideas inspired many novels, such as *Frankenstein*, by Mary Wollstonecraft Shelley.

One of Leonardo da Vinci's most famous works had to do with human anatomy. It is called the *Vitruvian Man*, and it is a sketch of a human male. The drawing shows a man standing up straight with his arms outstretched, inside of a perfect square. This helped the idea that the arms-width of a human being is equal to the height of a human. If the male is in a perfect square, then the two must be equal. The drawing also shows additional arms and legs coming off the human body, but the arms and legs are at a diagonal. These limbs fit exactly on the edges of a perfect circle, showing that the human body is proportional.

The *Vitruvian Man* sketch shows that Leonardo knew the dimensions—the height, the width, the length—of the human body. His expertise was unparalleled at the time. So why do we care, though? What is so important about these drawings that were put onto paper hundreds of years ago?

Well, as the years go on, we become more knowledgeable. Every single day, scientists and doctors are making life-changing discoveries and ideas, ones that will change our lives. But our progress started hundreds of years ago, with men like Leonardo da Vinci, who could observe the world around them and make the world a better place. From Leonardo, the world gained new information about human beings. You could say that Leonardo changed the way that we look at ourselves. He thought of us as machines that could be studied. His work changed the world, and changed history and science forever.

Chapter 6: The Mona Lisa

Perhaps you have heard of it—Leonardo da Vinci's *Mona Lisa*, one of the most famous paintings in the entire world. Each year, millions of people flock to Paris so that they can catch a glimpse of it. When you first take a look at the painting, you may think that it is boring and plain. After all, it is just a painting of a woman. What is so remarkable about it?

For centuries, historians and scientists have been obsessed with discovering the identity of the woman in the painting. No one knows who she is, or how she knew Leonardo da Vinci. Were they friends? Were they family? Did she actually exist at all, or was she someone that Leonardo invented?

During Leonardo da Vinci's time period, it was decidedly uncommon for people to have their portrait drawn. Today, we have cameras, and we can take pictures of whatever we want whenever we like. But hundreds of years ago, only the rich and famous citizens could afford to have themselves drawn. So, we know that, if the *Mona Lisa* is, in fact, a real person, she was either extremely wealthy, or terribly important to Leonardo da Vinci. Portraits were not easy to paint, especially one so precise and beautiful as Leonardo's *Mona Lisa*. The person in a painting would usually need to sit or stand for hours, sometimes more than a *day*, before the artist finished.

Other things about the painting make it abundantly intriguing. For one, the woman in the painting is wearing all black—and it was very common for *widows*—women whose husbands had died—to wear black. Many people have also pointed out the landscape on the left of the woman is slightly higher than the landscape on the right; did Leonardo, who was such a brilliant and precise artist, do this on purpose? And, if she was a wealthy woman, why is she not wearing any jewelry in the painting?

When one looks at the woman's hand and face, it is possible to see how lifelike she is. This is partially the reason why the painting became so famous. Very few painters were able to capture such a lifelike image—to paint a person who looked so real. Leonardo da Vinci loved his painting so much that, when he completed it, he took it everywhere with him. Most likely, he had been hired by the woman's husband to paint the picture—but ended up keeping it. It truly is a fantastic design!

So, who is the mysterious woman that Leonardo painted?

The woman in the painting also has a smile on her face, but the smile looks suspicious, almost as if she is hiding a secret. Is she smiling at a joke? Does she know something that we don't know? The possibilities are nearly endless. One theory suggests that the woman is merely the wife of a wealthy merchant and that she is happy to see him. But other ideas get crazier and crazier.

Some people theorize that the *Mona Lisa* could have been Salai. Other ideas state that the woman in the painting is actually Leonardo himself. It was common in Leonardo's day for artists to leave behind a self-portrait—a drawing of themselves. But Leonardo did not do this; so many people speculate that the *Mona Lisa* could actually be a self-portrait.

Really, there is no way that we can know the truth, and many people like it this way. The mystery behind the *Mona Lisa* is partially the reason why we still study it today, and why millions of people visit it in the Louvre museum in France. We want to know more about one of the most brilliant and enigmatic people to ever walk the Earth, and the *Mona Lisa* could be a brilliant insight. Despite the continued mystery, however, some experts think that they know the truth.

It is becoming popular opinion that the "Lisa" in the painting is Lisa Gherardini, also known as Lisa del Giocondo, who lived across the street from Leonardo da Vinci at approximately the time he was painting the portrait. In 2012, scientists opened a tomb in Florence—a tomb that was thought to be the burial site of Lisa Gherardini. After doing some DNA testing, the scientists determined that one of the bodies inside was, in fact, Lisa Gherardini. Once the scientists had her DNA, they used a computer to recreate an image of what her face would look like. The results were extremely close to the woman portrayed in Leonardo da Vinci's *Mona Lisa.* But even despite some pretty convincing evidence, there are plenty of people who hold to their strange ideas.

The famous painting can be found at the *Louvre* Museum in Paris, France. The museum is known for its staggering assortment of old art and architecture. It is arguably one of the most famous museums in the entire world. In 1911, an employee stole the painting in the middle of the day—and it went missing for two years! Some historians say that this is part of why the painting is so famous today. If a work by a popular historical figure were to go missing, it might suddenly become famous as people wonder where it is. The *Mona Lisa* was found in 1913, and it was returned to the Louvre.

Over the centuries, the paint on the *Mona Lisa* has peeled and worn away. Some people have even attempted to break it by throwing rocks at it. Now, though, the *Mona Lisa* is safely protected inside of the Louvre. Visitors might be surprised by the peeling paint and the varnish on the design. Many scientists and art experts have attempted to recreate the painting as Leonardo da Vinci had originally imagined it.

Recently, scientists believe that the painting currently inside the Louvre is not even the work created by Leonardo da Vinci, but instead created by one of his apprentices, possibly even his friend and apprentice Salai. Whether this is true or not is unknown. A family in Geneva, Switzerland has also come forward, claiming that they have a painting of the *Mona Lisa* from several years before Leonardo da Vinci's famous work was created. One thing is clear, though: people around the world have been obsessed with the *Mona Lisa* for centuries, and we will continue to be so. There is something about the painting, some fascinating aspect, that makes people constantly recreate it, parody it, and write about it. It is arguably Leonardo da Vinci's most famous and well-known work, as well as the most famous painting in the history of the world.

Some people claim that it took Leonardo da Vinci ten years to paint just the lips of the woman in the painting. Is this true? Well, we can't know for sure. But we know that the lips and the eyes of the woman are perhaps the most interesting part of the painting, since both seem to say that the woman is hiding something. When Leonardo da Vinci painted the *Mona Lisa*, he did not outline the shapes first. Instead, he used only think brushstrokes (which you can see if you look extremely carefully) and mixed colors together to create the painting.

The *Mona Lisa* became Leonardo's most treasured painting, and also the most famous painting in the world. Leonardo da Vinci took the *Mona Lisa* with him everywhere, and he often called it his greatest accomplishment.

Chapter 7: Leonardo Leads the Renaissance

Leonardo created many of his most famous works during a time period known as the *Renaissance*. The Renaissance was a period of three hundred and fifty years, during which Europe exploded with astonishing advancements in art, architecture, and creative and logical thinking. Renaissance stands for the word "rebirth." People call this period the *Renaissance* because it was a "rebirth" of many of the ideas and cultural works that had been crucial to Ancient Greek and Roman society. The Greeks and Romans were known for their gorgeous and unique architecture, as well as their paintings.

Why did the Renaissance start? Well, before the Renaissance, many Europeans had marched into the Middle East to fight a war known as the "Crusades." The Crusades were fought over different religious opinions. But despite the petty fighting, Europeans came into contact with rich Middle Eastern cultures and brought many new ideas back to Europe with them. These ideas ignited a creative fire that would become known as the Renaissance.

Leonardo was one of the key artists of the Renaissance, inspired by many famous painters and thinkers before him. The Renaissance stretched from the year 1350 to 1700, and Leonardo lived from 1452 to 1519.

Leonardo da Vinci, though, competed with many other artists for fame and popularity. In particular, there are three other names you might memorize: Raphael, Michelangelo, and Donatello. It is not a coincidence that the Teenage Mutant Ninja Turtles' names are those three plus Leonardo—they were named after four of the most famous artists of the Renaissance!

Raphael was a terrific artist. At the ripe age of twenty-one, when Leonardo was already well on his way to fame, Raphael was in Florence. In fact, Raphael loved to study Leonardo da Vinci's works. To him, Leonardo was an inspiration and a model of what he could become some day. Like Leonardo, Raphael also drew many paintings that had to do with Christianity, including many about the Virgin Mary and Jesus as a baby. He also drew many scenes from Ancient Greece. Since the Renaissance used many ideas from Ancient Greece and Rome, it made sense that people suddenly wanted to recreate paintings of the most famous Greek and Roman thinkers, such as Socrates, Plato, and Aristotle.

Michelangelo, on the other hand, was not too much of a painter. In fact, he loved to build sculptures and use his hands to mold his art. His most famous sculpture is *David*, who was a character in the Bible. According to the story, David fought the giant beast Goliath and survived. Because of this amazing story, many paintings showed David after the battle, often standing over the severed head of the beast. But Michelangelo wanted to show David before the battle—and he ended up creating an almost perfect representation of the human body. The statue stands at over fourteen feet tall—imagine seeing a fourteen-foot tall statue of a human being! *David*'s muscles are tense, and his pose is heroic. People from around the world flocked to see the beautiful sculpture of the Biblical hero. It inspired many religious people and brought life to scenes from the Bible.

You also might know that Michelangelo painted the entire ceiling of the Sistine Chapel. The Sistine Chapel is the Pope's chapel in Rome. The ceiling is absolutely beautiful, and one of the most impressive artistic feats ever created.

Leonardo da Vinci and Michelangelo had a fierce rivalry with each other. For starters, Leonardo had spent a goodly amount of his life as a lowly apprentice, working his way up to fame. Michelangelo had always been rich, but he still dressed messily and was not clean. Leonardo, on the other hand, knew that he needed to look nice and have a neat appearance. Michelangelo had grown up jealous of Leonardo. He had been born when Leonardo da Vinci was already twenty-seven years old, and famous.

Leonardo da Vinci told people that he thought Michelangelo's gorgeous statue of *David* was unimpressive—merely the work of an amateur. Whether Leonardo secretly admired *David* we will never know. What we do know is that Leonardo was highly likely jealous. Leonardo's horse sculpture that he had tried to build in Milan had been a complete disaster and destroyed by the French army, yet Michelangelo's *David* sculpture was famous across the world.

The two men would often argue, fight, and even compete for fame. When both Leonardo da Vinci and Michelangelo were staying in Florence, they were called upon for an art competition: each of them was to paint part of the government building's wall, depicting famous battles of Florence. Leonardo had no trouble thinking about a design. He wanted to make the battle so real that people in the room felt like they were in it.

However, the painting had to be on a wall, so it was considered a *fresco*, and the last fresco Leonardo had done was *The Last Supper*. He did not like painting in the traditional fresco way, and his wall ended up a complete mess. It was a painting disaster, one that completely embarrassed him. However, Michelangelo never ended up finishing his fresco, since he was called to Rome to paint the ceiling of the Sistine Chapel. Perhaps Leonardo was happy that this happened. It saved him even more embarrassment. He was adept at many things, but frescoes were not his specialty.

Chapter 8: Later in Life

To help his artistic ideas, Leonardo spent much of his time in different cities. In the year 1504, when he was in Florence with Michelangelo, Leonardo da Vinci's father passed away at an amazing seventy-eight years old, which was quite a long lifespan for the time. Ser Piero, his father, had left no will whatsoever, and all of Ser Piero's other children received his money and belongings. Leonardo da Vinci was left with nothing.

He still had his fame and his fortune, though, but he suffered another loss when his Uncle Francesco died three years later. This was a harder hit for Leonardo since Francesco had been like a father to him for most of his life. Francesco left all of his money, his belongings, and his land to Leonardo—but Leonardo's half-siblings were extremely upset about this.

Leonardo was forced to leave Milan and travel to Florence so that he could fix the problems with his siblings. They all went to court. The courts decided that Leonardo would be able to use Francesco's lands but that he did not own them. Instead, when he died, the lands would go to Leonardo's half-siblings. When all the trouble was over, Leonardo eagerly left Florence and returned to Milan.

He did not stay there for too long though. When the year 1513 rolled around, Leonardo da Vinci traveled to the Rome and stayed at the Vatican. His counterparts Raphael and Michelangelo were both staying in Rome as well, which could have been awkward for everyone, especially since Leonardo and Michelangelo did not say goodbye on a good note. Leonardo was still angry over their fresco contest.

When he was at the Vatican, which is the home of the Catholic Pope, Leonardo da Vinci met Francis I. Francis I was the King of France at the time and, despite the fact that Leonardo and Francis I were from two countries that had warred with each other, they got along remarkably well. Francis I loved Leonardo's company, and he invited Leonardo to stay with him. Leonardo happily agreed.

He moved from Milan to the northern France city of Amboise in 1516. Leonardo loved it there. The city was beautiful, surrounded by terrific landscapes and friendly people. Leonardo could not bring too many of his belongings such a far distance, so he needed to choose carefully. He ultimately decided that he would need to take the *Mona Lisa*, his personal favorite. With him also came his vast assortment of books.

Francis I asked Leonardo to build a robotic lion that could walk forward, and whose chest would burst open to reveal a small group of lily flowers. Leonardo successfully created the lion, which used gears and cranks to slowly move forward. It was an astounding sight to see, and Francis I was more than impressed.

Recently, five hundred years after Leonardo da Vinci created the mechanical lion, historians and scientists have recreated it, just in the way that da Vinci did. The lion was rebuilt in northern France, since this is where Leonardo spent his final years.

Francis I and Leonardo got along great. Every day, the King of France and Leonardo da Vinci would discuss a variety of topics. The king loved to hear how Leonardo's mind worked, and he loved the way Leonardo would talk. Da Vinci was one of the greatest minds of his time, so it's no wonder that King Francis I enjoyed his company so much.

But it did not last too long. Leonardo da Vinci died on May 2nd, 1519. There are many rumors surrounding his death, and there is no way of telling if they are true or not. One of the more popular rumors states that, when Leonardo died, King Francis I held him in his arms. A painting called "Death of Leonardo da Vinci," created by Jean-Auguste-Dominique Ingres depicts the dramatic death, although he may have exaggerated it a bit.

Some people also say that Leonardo da Vinci's final words were about his horse sculpture—the disastrous sculpture that he never completed and that the French soldiers used as target practice.

Leonardo da Vinci was buried in the Chapel of Saint-Hubert, which is part of the French castle that King Francis ruled. But who received all of Leonardo's personal belongings?

Leonardo's friend and apprentice, Francesco Melzi, had been staying with him in Amboise. He received all the money that Leonardo had made over the years, as well as Leonardo's paintings, his painting supplies, and all of his books. And what about Salai? Well, Salai was given a portion of Leonardo's vineyards.

Leonardo was mourned by people around the world. They truly felt as if they had lost the greatest mind of their generation. His sculptures, his paintings, his sketches would be remembered for more than half of a millennium to come—and still, we celebrate the life of Leonardo da Vinci. His artwork and his mind are unparalleled, and he still stands as possibly the most celebrated and accomplished artist of all time.

But what is it exactly that makes us so fascinated with him and his life?

Chapter 9: Leonardo In Our World Today

There are milions of artists out there today, but still we decide to worship Leonardo da Vinci. He lived five hundred years ago, his paintings are old and falling apart, half of his notebook pages are missing, and many of his sculptures and machines, are no longer surviving. There were dozens of renowned artists living at the time that we could be studying. So *what makes Leonardo da Vinci so astounding?*

If Leonardo da Vinci had been born later in life, he may have not been so famous. It was because Leonardo was born during the Renaissance that his paintings take on a whole new meaning. He worked during an era of change. People were beginning to think different, and the world was becoming more modern and up-to-date. The 1400s and 1500s were a period of enormous transition, and Leonardo da Vinci was part of this.

Through his artwork, he helped people see differently. If you look at the *Mona Lisa*, you see a wonderful portrait of a mysterious woman. The painting itself carries a decidedly eerie feeling, almost as if Lisa del Giacondo is staring directly at you, across five hundred years of history and hundreds of miles. Before Leonardo's paintings, very few people were able to recreate such like-like images. The people that went, and still go, to see his paintings feel as if they are looking at something real, as if they are looking into another world right before their eyes.

Never before had viewers of paintings been so touched. In the world of art, the relationship between a painting and the audience is a very important one. The artist needs to attract the viewer, and Leonardo da Vinci was a master of this. Audiences from around the world still flock to see his paintings—not just because they are historically famous, but because they are unique. They are something amazing that a human being has created. He did not merely paint for himself—he painted for all of humanity.

Leonardo was such a genius because he was a merging point for both the arts, science, and nature. He observed the world around him and absorbed everything that he saw. He saw the world as an incredibly fascinating place, one that held untold wonders. He needed to put life onto the painting, as a way of giving back to life, and showing people the beauty of art.

In order to study how things worked, Leonardo da Vinci *looked* at them. Whether he was capturing birds so that he could observe their flight pattern, sketching every little detail of his favorite flower, and dissecting a human body so that he could see the inside, Leonardo was a prime example of the world's best scientist. All of his ideas were hundreds of years ahead of his time, and the airplane is a great example of this. Leonardo was a man of many ideas—some ideas that would not be fulfilled until four hundred years after his death.

The Renaissance was a transition period in which undeveloped countries started to learn more and more about the world around them. Leonardo da Vinci helped people learn, and he helped people understand the world. Just as important as the world, he changed the way that people think about people. When he drew human body parts, he drew them with knowledge that people had rarely ever seen before. He did not just see a hand; he saw a wild mix of muscles, bones, veins, and skin. He did not just see a leg, he saw a piece of machinery that could pivot at the knee and carry humans forward.

Leonardo da Vinci was a *symbol* of the Renaissance, and he is often called the "Renaissance man." Why? Because he stood for everything that the Renaissance was. He was an inventor, and many people at the time were creating new inventions that could be used to make the world easier. Many of these inventions had to do with warfare, since guns were making appearances at the time. Would soldiers still fight with swords? How could humans create the best guns? How many bullets could you fire? How long would it take to reload? Would cannons still be used to take down castles? Leonardo da Vinci did plenty of work in creating new weapons that could be used in castle sieges. He was so brilliant, and for this reason many dukes and kings wanted him for themselves. If you were a king at the time, you would want Leonardo da Vinci to work for you!

If Leonardo da Vinci had never existed, our society may not be as advanced as it is today. Think about it: Leonardo da Vinci created the ideas for the first airplane. The Wright Brothers used his designs in the early 1900s to create the first plane. The Wright Brothers' plane led to the use of planes in war, and for us to have millions of flights crossing the world each day. What would have happened if Leonardo da Vinci had never created that design? Would we still have airplanes?

Well, most likely, but we may have developed them at a much slower pace, and they may not have been as advanced. Leonardo da Vinci changed the course of human history forever, and that is one of the reasons that we must study him, if we want to understand how our world works.

He showed us that we can be experts at many things at the same time. Leonardo loved to play music, he loved to draw, he liked to take things apart and rebuild them, he loved to paint, and he enjoyed thinking about the world. His paintings show us how he thought about the world, and also how the world was like during the Renaissance.

It is funny to know that Leonardo da Vinci was often disappointed in himself. He thought that he did not always meet expectations, and that his work was not that great. One of these examples is the failed fresco contest with his rival, Michelangelo. But Leonardo truly had no reason to be disappointed. When he died at the age of sixty-seven, which was a decent age for a person to live to at the time, he had accomplished than most people in the world would ever create.

For hundreds of years, and even still today, people look up to Leonardo da Vinci. They see his paintings and are inspired by his artistic ability and his brilliance. He was a source of inspiration for many poor people too, since he started out pretty poor. He was only able to succeed because his father helped him—but even then, Leonardo's persistence and his imagination were what truly made him famous. He could never have created the *Mona Lisa* or *The Last Supper* if he had not started out by drawing in a sketchbook.

Today, as we look around, we may see planes flying across the sky. We see bicycles speeding down the road. At the doctor's office, we may see posters of the human skeleton. Soon, we might even see robots on the streets! All of this is possible because of Leonardo da Vinci. His ideas for planes and bicycles and robots were not terribly advanced, but they were early blueprints. Later on, other people looked at Leonardo's notes and his papers, and saw all of the brilliant ideas he had. They took his ideas, and they made their own inventions so that we could make our world a better and more interesting place.

Leonardo da Vinci once wrote down in his notebooks: "The painter has the Universe in his minds and hands." This quotation shows why art is so crucial to the world, and why Leonardo da Vinci is so essential to history. Art is a way that people can see the world. Movies, books, and music are types of art, as well. Leonardo also said that poetry and paintings were the same thing, just in different shapes. Leonardo da Vinci was a master of art, so it is no wonder that people have followed his words of wisdom for centuries.

Many of Leonardo's most famous works sit in the Louvre Museum in Paris, France, and one of his paintings is even at a museum in America. One thing is for sure: we have loved Leonardo da Vinci for five hundred years, and we will continue to study his works and life for centuries to come.

Works By Da Vinci

The Annunciation (1472)

The Baptism of Christ (1475); created in cooperation with Raffael

Madonna of the Carnation (1478)

Portrait of Ginevra de' Benci (1474 - 1478)

Benois Madonna (1478)

The Adoration of the Magi (1480 - 1481)

St Jerome (1480)

Madonna Litta (1490)

Portrait of Musician Franchino Gaffurio (1490)

Lady with an Ermine (1490)

Virgin of the Rocks (1503 - 1506)

Last Supper (1495 - 1498)

Madonna with the Yarnwinder (1501)

Bibliography

"Art and Science. The Da Vinci Legacy." *Leonardo Da Vinci Legacy oi Ari ano Invention*. Italian Renaissance Art, n.d. Web. 25 Sept. 2013.

Boyle, Alan. "'Mona Lisa' Skeleton and Her Kin's Remains Are Due for DNA Testing."*NBC News*. National Broadcasting Company, 9 Aug. 2013. Web. 25 Sept. 2013.

Edwards, Roberta, and True Kelley. *Who Was Leonardo Da Vinci?* New York: Grosset & Dunlap, 2005. Print.

"Leonardo da Vinci." Encyclopædia Britannica. Encyclopædia Britannica Online Academic Edition. Encyclopædia Britannica Inc., 2013. Web. 25 Sep. 2013.

"Leonardo Da Vinci." Leonardo Da *Vinci*. Brookhaven National Laboratory, n.d. Web. 25 Sept. 2013.

"Leonardo Da Vinci Biography." *Leonardo Da Vinci Biography*. Www.leonardoda-vinci.org, n.d. Web. 25 Sept. 2013.

"Leonardo's "Mona Lisa"" *Mona Lisa*. Khan Academy, n.d. Web. 25 Sept. 2013.

"Leonardo's Vitruvian Man." *The Vitruvian Man*. Stanford University, n.d. Web. 25 Sept. 2013.

http://www.italian-renaissance-art.com/da-vinci-legacy.html

Pablo Picasso

Introdcution

Many famous artists lived hundreds of years ago. It seems that, in the past hundred and fifty years, only a small handful of artists have ever become remotely popular. Modern art just seems not to be as captivating as older art is. There are plenty of familiar names from hundreds of years ago—Leonardo da Vinci, Vincent van Gogh, Michelangelo, and Raphael, among many others.

One of the leaders of the modern art movement was named Pablo Picasso, a Spanish artist, many of whose paintings are still majorly famous and widely reprinted today. Picasso is known for his unique painting styles, and also his involvement in history. Picasso lived within the past century and a half, during which many drastic history movements were taking place, such as the Spanish Civil War, World War I, World War II, and many other cultural events that shaped the world as we know it. Part of the reason that Picasso is so famous is because the link between his art and history at the time.

In order to understand his art, we must first understand his life and what his childhood was like. How did he start painting? How did he decide what to put down on canvases and paper? What about his art made people like it? How did he become famous? What role did his art play during the times of World War I, World War II, and the Spanish Civil War? Why did he spend most of his life in France? What is his enduring legacy?

Pablo Picasso was an intriguing man that led a fascinating life, and studying him is studying a hugely important part of history and culture. Picasso's story is a human story, and many readers will find that he is one of the most intriguing artists in the world.

Chapter 1: Childhood of the Artist

In the south of Spain, there is a city called Malaga. Today, it is one of the most populated cities in all of Spain. At the time, among thousands of other people, there were two remarkable people living in Malaga: one of them was José Ruiz y Blasco and the other was María Picasso y López. José was a painter and a teacher, and he often taught young students how to draw. María and José married each other in 1880, and one year later they had their first child.

The child's name was exceptionally long: Pablo Diego Jose Prancisco de Paula Juan Nepomuceno Maria de los Remedios Cipriano de la Santisima Trinidad Ruiz y Picasso—or, for short, Pablo Picasso. Why were there so many names in Picasso's full name? During that time period, it was normal for parents to give their child several middle names, usually taken from family members or Catholic saints. Even today, the royal child born to Prince William and Duchess Kate Middleton was named George Alexander Louis. Although not as flashy as Picasso's name, in many families and cultures it is tradition for the names to be extra long.

Nether José nor María knew that one day, their child would grow up to be one of the most renowned artists in the entire world. Since José was an artist himself, he taught Pablo about drawing and painting from a remarkably young age. In fact, there is a story that says Pablo's first word was "*piz.*"

Piz is what babies who speak Spanish would first call a *lapiz*, which means "pencil" in Spanish. From the moment Pablo Picasso could pick up a pencil, he loved to draw. He would draw on paper, he would draw on dirt, he would draw in sand—it was something he loved to do, and his father was very, very proud of him.

Both José and María encouraged Pablo to become an artist from a remarkably young age. He showed promise, and it was something that he clearly loved to do. José liked to take Pablo to bullfights, which is a popular Spanish tradition. In an arena, a professional bullfighter takes on a bull; this can be a fearfully dangerous situation, so only very skilled people did it. The crowd loved to see these types of shows, and bullfighting is still popular in Spain today. The man often has to escape the bull, but he tries to do it in the most daring and exciting ways possible, to keep the audience entertained and to keep them coming back for more.

Pablo loved to see the bullfights with his father, and when he got home he tried to sketch out some of the scenes that he saw. When he was eight years old, he made an attempt at one of his very first paintings, which was about bullfighting. His mother and father were incredibly impressed, and they showed it to all of their family and friends, who told their family and friends, who told *their* family and friends, and soon, everyone was talking about the eight-year old artist named Pablo Picasso.

Pablo Picasso grew up with two siblings. One of them was named Lola, and the other was named Conchita. However, Conchita did not live for unusually long. When she was seven years old, she passed away from diphtheria, a breathing infection. Obviously, the entire family was devastated, although Pablo was not really old enough to understand. Despite his young age, though, he became afraid of death. He had seen death take his younger sister, and this made him afraid of death. If his sister had suffered death, couldn't anyone else be next?

Despite the death of Conchita and his fear, a young Pablo Picasso still managed to get his name out into the world as a successful artist. When he was thirteen years old, he held his first art show, which is when all of his works were showcased to an audience. Many people believe that his father José was incredibly jealous of Pablo's work; while José had been working all of his life for success, becoming an art teacher, Pablo was thirteen and already having art shows. Even if he was jealous, however, he was still incredibly proud. He passed all of his brushes and other utensils onto Pablo and never made any works of art ever again.

Pablo Picasso applied to art school the next year, something that was usually reserved for college students only. However, because he was so talented, he was immediately accepted into their program. This was also the school that José taught at, so it would be nice for José and Pablo to be in the same school. Pablo and his family moved to the Spanish city of Barcelona, which is currently the second largest city in all of Spain. It sits on the banks of the Mediterranean Sea, which makes it a hugely popular destination for tourists to visit.

At the school, Pablo Picasso quickly became a favorite among the professors there. They loved seeing his talent and his enthusiasm for art each day; he was one of the best students in the entire school! At age fourteen, he was taking classes for only the most advanced artists, and he managed to keep a decent pace throughout the class. Pablo was talented way beyond his years.

When he was sixteen years old, he created a work of art called *Science and Charity*, which depicted his sister Lola sick in bed, his father José at her side. There will be more details about this painting later, but it is essential to understand that the painting was put on display in the Spanish capital of Madrid, where it won a truly special award! Pablo Picasso had not even reached eighteen years old, and yet he was still famous across the country of Spain. His artwork was placed beside the works of Spain's greatest artists; his talents compared with those who had worked with a brush for decades.

After *Science and Charity* was awarded in Madrid, José and María knew that their son could not remain in Barcelona. He was too talented. He had too bright of a future ahead of him—he needed to go somewhere else, to study among the greats, to show his true potential in the adult world. So where were they going to send him?

There was no better place than Madrid, a center for arts and science and culture in Spain. Pablo was sent to the Royal Academy of San Fernando, one of the most renowned schools in the entire country. However, as great of an artist as Pablo was, he was not the greatest student.

Pablo Picasso did not always attend each of his classes. Instead, he would skip them, which was against the rules. He also did not like the way that they thought art at the school. Many of his teachers made him copy notable examples from art history, which was a method that had been used for centuries. The teachers thought that, by copying examples from ancient history, the students would learn what good art really was. Pablo, however, disagreed with this idea.

Pablo wanted to learn by painting his own ideas and trying out different styles of art. This method, after all, was what led to such great success with many of his early paintings. He loved studying history and ancient artists and their work, but he also wanted to be independent from them. So, that was exactly what he would do.

However, Pablo Picasso did not last terribly long at the school. It was unfortunate timing; the next winter, he became sick with scarlet fever, which had infected many people at the time. He came down with a seriously sore throat and rashes across his body. He had to take time off from school while he was sick, and during this time he thought about what the future might hold for him.

When he became better, did he *really* want to return to art school? No, not really. He did not like it there. He did not like the teachers, and he did not like the way that they ran the class. The Royal Academy of San Fernando was just not the place for him. He was Pablo Picasso, and he was going to paint things the way he wanted to. His family expressed their disagreement; the Royal Academy was one of the best schools in all of Spain; how could he just throw away his education?

Pablo was not sorry for his decision. He was not going to let a school control his art. He was going to make his way out into the world and paint his own future.

Chapter 2: Picasso Explores the World

By the time that Picasso was nineteen years old, he was off on his own. His boring school life was behind him, and the world was in front of him, ready to be explored! He decided that he would actually like to return to Barcelona, since he had liked it so much more than Madrid. It was in Barcelona that Picasso became part of something called the Modernist movement—artists who painted things differently than they had ever been painted before.

One of the centers for the Modernist movement was a café called The Four Cats. Cafes were often breeding centers for art and culture, and at any time, one could find innovative artists inside. Pablo loved spending time inside The Four Cats, or, as it was officially called Els Quatre Gats in the language of Catalan, which is a variation of Spanish. Since The Four Cats was hugely supportive of growing artists in Spain, they let Pablo show off his work to many of the customers, who thought his art was fantastic. They had never seen anything like it!

And that was when the opportunity of a lifetime came. One of Pablo's paintings was about to make him world famous when officials in Paris, France decided that it was good off to be showcased at the World's Fair. The World's Fair is a collection of works from all across the world, and it is held in a different city and country every year. It was extremely convenient that this year, it was in Paris, France—just one country away from Spain. It would not be truly far for Pablo to travel.

But Pablo was not just excited about showing his art off to famous people from across the world—he was excited to explore! He had never been to Paris before, and he knew that, in the city, he would experience all new things. Paris was known around the world as one of the most popular places for artists to travel to.

He did not want to go to Paris alone, so he asked one of his old friends from art school to join him. His friend's name was Carles Casagemas, and he was just as excited as Pablo to live in Paris and explore the marvellous city.

Without wasting any time, Pablo and Carles were soon off to Paris, France. Paris is the capital of France, and it is most well known for the Eiffel Tower (along with its delicious French food!). Pablo and Carles shared an apartment together, but they did not have enough money to pay for an expensive, adequate apartment. Instead, they had an apartment where the walls were bare and blank. They did not have any money for furniture or any accessories, and they both thought that their apartment was abundantly plain.

Pablo decided that he would put his artistic talent to work. On the walls around the apartment, he painted tables, chairs, bookcases, and other furniture items, so that it looked like they had stuff around their apartment. During the night, Pablo and Carles slept peacefully in their homely apartment—by day, the two of them explored the wondrous city that is Paris.

All around Paris, there was plenty of art to see. Van Gogh had died ten years ago, and people around the world were beginning to become fascinated with his art—including Pablo Picasso. Paris was a place of inspiration for him. He visited museums and art shows and was inspired by all of the great works that he saw; he saw the Parisian countryside and lovely city and was taken aback by its beauty. He would often paint things that he saw in Paris, since he loved the city so much.

Pablo's time in Paris did not last terribly long. After Pablo had shown his art off to the world, the excitement in his life died down. He wished once again to see his homeland of Spain, and so did Carles, who had been enduring tough times apart from his girlfriend. When his girlfriend left Carles for good, Pablo and Carles decided that it was time to move back to Spain.

Despite the fact that Pablo Picasso had been having an incredible time in Paris, France, his family was quite skeptical of his progress. When he returned home to visit his parents, his hair was long, and he was dressed fancily, like many of the Parisians. His parents were afraid that his work was making him forget his Spanish heritage. Would he still become the celebrated painter they thought he would be? Sure, his artwork had just been displayed in Paris— but what would happen next?

Because he did not want to disappoint his mother and father, he moved from Barcelona back to Madrid. Each day, he kept up painting and drawing for practice. He worked for magazines, he worked for newspapers—until something terrible happened.

Carles, Pablo's best friend, had been having a very hard time. He was depressed and distraught and eventually committed suicide over a broken heart. Pablo was horrified over the event; it was totally unexpected. Pablo was especially sad that, in Carles's final days and months, he had not been very present as a friend.

Carles's death had a profound impact on Pablo Picasso's life. Pablo started to paint with many more blue colors. Why is this so important? What does the color blue mean in a painting? This is crucial to understand, especially if you want to understand hidden meanings in art. Blue is a color that is typically associated with sadness, so people knew that something was wrong in his life.

To deal with his sorrow, Pablo painted some pictures of Carles. They were all heavily tainted with the color blue, and Pablo even admitted that there was a clear link between the use of the color blue in his art and Carles. Many historians even call this time in Pablo Picasso's life the "Blue Period," since he used the color so much. It is no coincidence that the color "blue" also means "sad" or "feeling down."

Pablo was unsure of what to do next, now that Carles was gone. He spent a lot of time traveling back and forth between cities, mainly Paris and Barcelona. He could not afford consistent homes, so he often found himself living in either inadequate hotels—either that, or apartments that were old and unsafe.

Once again, Pablo genuinely wanted someone to live with—so he asked another one of his artist friends to live with him. His name was Max Jacobs, and he specialized in writing poetry. Both Pablo and Max were working to make a hard living as artists—Pablo often had to work overnight because there simply weren't enough hours in the day.

Pablo was running out of money. He did not have the money to find a steady home, and he most certainly did not have the money to purchase enough proper art supplies. While many painters used canvases to take down their work, Pablo did not have enough money. He had to use paper instead of canvases.

So, what types of things did Picasso like to paint? The poor and the disabled interested Picasso, so he would often paint them. He would paint homeless people that he found living on the streets of Paris and Barcelona. He would visit prisons and paint and draw images of the prisoners.

During this time in Picasso's life, he was terribly sad. His best friend had died, and interest in his art was lacking. People were not buying his art like he thought they would; sure, his art had been displayed in Paris. But something was wrong—if his art was so good, why were people not buying it? Pablo's parents were convinced that it had something to do with his time spent in Paris. They told him that he should not paint any more blue paintings; obviously, people did not want to buy them.

Chapter 3: Picasso Grows Into An Artist

No matter what people thought of him and his art, Pablo Picasso continued to do what he thought was right. Who cares if people didn't like his blue paintings? Who cares if his parents thought his career was going downhill? Eventually, things started to look a bit brighter for Picasso—in his life, and in his art.

He realized that he *really* liked Paris—way better than Barcelona. Paris was just such an amazing center of art and culture. It is impossible to deny Paris's importance in Picasso's life since it had such a profound impact and influence on his art. He decided that he wanted to stay in Paris—but not just temporarily. He wanted to live there permanently, he liked it so much. He knew that Paris was the city that would change his life, that would truly make him happy.

If you compare Picasso's paintings when he was traveling to his paintings when he was living in Paris, there is a noticeable difference. Not only do his later paintings contain more bright and lively colors, but they just seem happier. It is almost as if the viewer can see Picasso's smiling, focused face looking at his work as he determinedly makes each brushstroke.

If Pablo Picasso had just been living in a time that historians call the "Blue Period," he was now living in the "Rose Period," since the color of a rose is much happier color. It is also appropriate that the rose is a symbol of love, for Picasso's love life was also looking up. Although he had never had too much luck and experience with the ladies, he found great partnership in Fernande Olivier, who was a fellow artist. Picasso she thought she was absolutely gorgeous, and the two of them got along together.

Pablo and Fernande could think of no place better to live in Paris, in a large apartment house that was full of other artists. Even though the house was not in the best shape, and even though it was falling apart in some places, Pablo and Fernande were happy where they were.

All of the artists inside the apartment house were excited to be living with *the* Pablo Picasso. He was something of a rising star as his paints become more and more famous. He was coming along, slowly but surely. But his paintings were not the only thing that made him an intriguing person.

Pablo Picasso was very smart. He liked to have interesting, intellectual discussions that involved a lot of thought and wonder. By no means was he a boring person. Everyone loved talking with him and being around him. They genuinely felt like he was one of the important people of the time; little did they know, Pablo Picasso's art would go on to change the world.

There were two people in particular that recognized the importance of Pablo Picasso's work. The Steins, a pair of siblings from America, instantly became great friends with Picasso. The brother's name was Leo Stein, and the sister's name was Gertrude Stein. The Steins loved art just as much as Picasso did, and they always invited artists over for dinner. When they invited Picasso to their house, he was absolutely thrilled. He felt like a celebrity!

But it did not end there. At the Steins' house, Picasso met his idol. He met Henri Matisse, one of the most famous artists of the time period, and Picasso's favorite painter. It was the equivalent of, today, a child meeting their favorite movie star or television show character. Pablo Picasso was instantly enthralled; he had met his favorite painter of all time, who had inspired much of his work and convinced him to keep on painting, no matter what.

Henri Matisse, as well, instantly took a liking to the young and enthusiastic Pablo Picasso. Since the two of them were artists, they competed with each other for fame and money—just like two bands or two television shows might compete against each other today. However, despite this, Matisse and Picasso recognized the brilliance of each other's work and shared an uncommonly deep friendship.

At one of these dinner events, Pablo and Gertrude Stein agreed that he would attempt to create a painting of her. Surely this would be absolutely no trouble for the talented and skilled Picasso. However, the painting ended up being much more of a challenge than he had originally thought. He messed up on the face once and started over—and then he messed up again and started over—and then he messed up again—he did this eighty times. Picasso was flustered, and even Gertrude Stein was becoming slightly impatient.

Eventually, Picasso finished Gertrude's portrait, but he was decidedly displeased with his work. Did this really look like her? Would people like his painting? Would people think that he was a poor painter and never want to buy his art again? Many of Picasso's followers thought that the painting bore remarkably little resemblance to Gertrude, but Gertrude was not so critical. She told him that she loved it—she had such an interest in the young Picasso that she probably would have liked anything he had drawn.

This led Picasso to a very important realization. He had tried eighty times to paint Gertrude Stein's face—why did he keep on failing? How could he become better? Was it skill that needed work, or was it his perspective? A *perspective* is the way in which someone looks at something. Picasso realized that he was having so much trouble with Gertrude's portrait because he was trying to get every single little detail to be painted as accurately as possible. But what if things did not *need* to be that way? What if he could paint what he saw in his *mind*, and not what he saw with his *eyes*?

Picasso changed the way he painted, and this led to a huge success in his art career. He was no longer focused on the details, and this allowed him to expand his creativity. He enjoyed painting much more, and people enjoyed his work much more too. It was a win-win situation! The money was pouring in, which made him and Fernande supremely happy. They were able to afford more things, live in a better, adequate house, and even go on scenic vacations. However, their relationship did not last much longer. Picasso was enticed by Fernande's beauty, but he no longer liked her as a person. It was not long before he had a new girlfriend.

As Picasso's personal life was changing, so was his artistic career. He liked to explore different artistic methods and techniques with many of the artists that he hung around with. One of his greatest friends was a man by the name of Georges Braque. Together, Picasso and Braque invented a technique of art that is used in schools across the country and across the world. Perhaps you have even done this yourself! It is called a "collage." The word "collage" is a French word that means "to stick."

Picasso and Braque would occasionally paste items onto their paintings, such as texts from newspapers and magazines. Instead of painting certain things, they thought that using real-world items would send a greater message and truly make their work come alive. Now, collages are made in classrooms and in workplaces across the world—all thanks to Pablo Picasso and Georges Braque!

Chapter 4: Picasso Steps Onto the World Stage

Picasso lived during a hugely important time in the world's history—he saw World War I erupt across the globe as countries pointed fingers at each other, took sides, made allies, and declared war. A man from Serbia assassinated Archduke Franz Ferdinand from Austria, and soon enough, Serbia and Austria were at each other's throats. The large country of Russia wanted to protect Serbia's actions, while Germany immediately flew to Austria's side. Germany was incensed by Russia; how could they possibly take Serbia's side? So Germany issued an official declaration of war on Russia.

So how was Picasso involved in all of this? Well, after France issued a statement declaring its support for Serbia and Russia, Germany declared war on France too. It was not long before the United States of America, along with several other countries around the world, were dragged into the conflict. The entire world was at war with itself for the first time.

This all happened in the year 1914, when Picasso and Braque were still living in France. While the war did not have an enormous and immediate effect on Picasso, it did have a vital part to play in Braque's life. The French government issued a *draft*, which is when they force citizens to join the military. The United States has not issued a draft since the 1970s during the Vietnam War, and the whole idea of a draft has become generally unpopular. But World War I and World War II saw many drafts and France was one country that supported them.

Braque was forced into the military, but Picasso was not. Why not? Picasso was technically not a French citizen, so the French government could not force him to serve in their army. While Braque and many of Picasso's friends went off to fight Germany and Austria, Picasso remained in France.

The war raised some truly interesting questions in France. For starters, the man that owned a gallery with Picasso's work in it was a German man. France was at war with Germany, so they immediately saw the gallery owner as an enemy and a potential spy. The French government wanted to take no chances, so they deported him and took all of the art inside the gallery—this included many of Picasso's famous pieces of art.

As Picasso saw the world around him falling apart, so too did his love life fall apart. His new girlfriend, Eva Gouel, came down with a terrible sickness called tuberculosis. While today there may be many medicines and treatments that a person can take for tuberculosis, at the start of the twentieth century, medicine was not as advanced. Unfortunately, Eva passed away, leaving Picasso absolutely devastated.

His friends were all away at war, and he was at home alone. His girlfriend had just died. Things were not going well in Picasso's life, and this once again reflected in his paintings. Picasso was sad, but he hoped that things would eventually get better.

He did not spent the entirety of World War I stuck in Paris, France, however. He actually traveled to Rome, a very famous city in Italy! While in Paris, he met a poet by the name of Jean Cocteau, who had risen to fame because his work was so likable and relatable. Like most people, Jean Cocteau adored Pablo Picasso. Cocteau knew that Picasso was extremely intelligent, very creative, and very friendly as well—despite the war raging to the east, and the effect it had on Picasso.

Jean Cocteau wanted to work on something with Picasso, but painting was not actually his expertise. Cocteau had been working with a ballet lately, and he thought it would be fantastic if Picasso could help out! When Picasso asked what the play was called and what it was about, Cocteau told him that it was called "Parade," and that it was about an extravagant circus!

Picasso immediately saw that he could be exceptionally creative with this project, and that was something that he liked. He had some doubts though, especially because he had never even seen a ballet before in his lifetime. Still, he took the challenge on. It would give him a chance to do something other than painting, and he would be able to travel to Rome!

Picasso's part in the project was to design the costumes and the set pieces for the ballet. He thought he did an excellent job, and he could not wait for people to see his work!

When opening night came, both Picasso and Cocteau were incredibly nervous. What would people think? Would they like the costumes? The play? After the first performance of the ballet, the audience was not too sure they liked it. The costumes were extravagant—a little *too* extravagant for the public's liking. It was like nothing they had ever seen before, and they did not like this. The play was overwhelming, so the general reaction was quite negative.

Obviously, Picasso and Cocteau were a little disappointed by this news, especially after how much effort they had put into creating the costumes and the set pieces. He decided that maybe ballets were not his area of expertise, so he decided to move away from them—however, there was something (or some*one*) about the ballet he could not get out of his mind.

It was a woman, and her name was Olga Khokhlova. She had been a dancer in the ballet, and throughout the entire experience, Picasso had absolutely fascinated with her beauty. He thought that she had been the most gorgeous ballet dancer in the entire production, and he revealed his interest in her. About one year after they had met each other, Pablo Picasso and Olga Khokhlova were married.

Olga was incredibly rich. She had friends in the high tiers of society. She always attended ballets and balls and wore all the newest fashions. People talked about her beauty and her riches. This was an incredibly different experience for Picasso. Just a few years ago, he was living in an apartment building that was falling apart, and now he was attending dances in fancy suits.

Pablo felt rather uncomfortable among the rich elite of Parisian society. All of his life, he had been a man of the poor and the working class. Many of his paintings depicted the lives of the homeless and those who struggled to survive—and here he was with more money than he knew what to do with, more food than he could eat, and more clothes than he could wear. Was this right for him to do?

A few years after Picasso and Olga got married, World War I ended with Germany and Austria standing disgraced and defeated, many other countries emerging as victors. Picasso was happy when all of his old friends returned home, but Olga did not like it when Picasso hung out with his friends. Many of them were not rich, and they were not proper; so why should her husband be with them? Picasso did not like it when she told him that, and, unfortunately, he went with the flow and did not see his friends as often.

It was not long before Olga became pregnant, and a new, smiling face joined their household. They named their new son Paulo when he was born in 1921. Pablo was the proudest father on the face of the earth, and he let everyone know. Several times he created paintings of Olga and Paulo together, happy.

Many people noticed a difference in his paintings of Olga and Paulo. We will talk more about this later, but most of Pablo Picasso's work tended to be hugely blocky, plain, and occasionally difficult to understand. His depictions of Olga and Paulo, however, were painted in much detail and truly lifelike.

For a while, things seemed to be going well for Pablo Picasso, despite the fact that he and Olga were not the best match. He could never get accustomed to her fancy way of living, and she was often rude to him. They eventually stopped sleeping together, and then she started criticizing his art and his studio. Picasso, like many famous artists, was not the most organized person, and his art studio was almost never neat. Picasso liked things like that, but Olga could not say the same. She kept on telling him to clean up his mess and, of course, he absolutely refused.

Enough was enough. Picasso had had enough of Olga, and he told her so when he purchased another house and left her. The house was still in Paris, although on the northern side, and Picasso hoped that it would be a decent enough escape for Olga. As had often happened with Picasso, it was not long before he had his sights set on someone else.

Marie-Therese Walter and Pablo Picasso had met in the Paris subway, and Picasso was instantly entranced with her. She was absolutely beautiful! As he had done with Olga and Paulo, Picasso enjoyed painting pictures of Marie-Therese. He simply could not get enough of her and, eventually, the two of them shared a daughter together. They named the girl Maya, and Picasso enjoyed painting pictures of her too.

But soon enough, another lady entered Picasso's life. Her name was Dora Maar, and she was a photographer. Picasso instantly fell in love with Dora, and soon he was faced with a predicament. He loved Marie-Therese, he loved Dora, and Olga was still trying to talk to him. What was he supposed to do? He now had two children with two different women. His problems were growing by the day, and he was not sure if there was any clear way out.

He decided that he wanted to be with Dora, but, after a while, he found that even his love for her was slowly dying. What was he supposed to do now? He met another woman, by the name of Françoise Gilot, who he *truly* fell in love with—hopefully. Picasso decided he liked her better than any of the other women, but how long that love would last no one could actually tell.

But, for the most part, it was very difficult for Picasso to focus on his love life. After all, he was alive at a time when the world was changing each and every day. Spain was erupting into a bloody civil battle, and the world was plunging into the climactic World War II.

Chapter 5: Picasso's World at War

After World War I, in the decade of the 1920s, Picasso spent most of his time in Paris. He experimented with different writing styles and dealt with his many romantic and family issues. This took up a lot of time and, about fifteen years later, in the year 1936, something terrible happened in Pablo Picasso's home country of Spain.

There was a military general, Francisco Franco, who overthrew the government, using the army to take the entire country hostage. Franco believed in a *fascist* government. *Fascism* is a type of government in which a single person—a *dictator*—controls everything in a country, and the people are not allowed to disagree with him. It is the opposite of freedom and liberty. The people of Spain were divided. Some people liked this new form of government, and others wanted to fight back against Franco and the Spanish army. Thus erupted the Spanish Civil War.

Under this form of government, and because battles were taking place throughout Spain each day, it was impossible for Picasso to go back home. It absolutely devastated him, and every single day he wished for the war to end and his people to be free.

The Spanish Civil War led to one of Picasso's most famous paintings. It was called *Guernica*, and perhaps you have even seen it before! There is a interesting story behind the painting.

In 1937, a year after the war had begun, Germany entered the war. Germany was under the rule of the fascist dictator Adolf Hitler, one of the villainous and infamous people in all of world history. Hitler had taken charge of Germany after World War I and saved the country of a horrible economic tragedy; the people of Germany loved Hitler for saving them; even though he made some bad decisions and prosecuted Jewish citizens, he was allowed to rise to the position of Fuhrer—the German word for "leader." In fact, Hitler is now considered to evil that the word "Fuhrer" is now defined as a tyrannous ruler.

German airplanes flew over the town of Guernica in northern Spain. No one had expected the attack, because there was no reason for Germany to interfere in Spain's civil war. The German planes soared over Guernica's streets and dropped bombs rapidly. Explosions erupted into the air, children and women and men screamed, animals ran everywhere, and entire buildings and roads were shattered to pieces.

The death count ran over one thousand six hundred people. Over nine hundred Spanish citizens suffered tough injuries. The Spanish rebellion was absolutely devastated; Franco and his German allies had won a great victory.

Picasso knew where Guernica was; it was even close to where he grew up as a child. He did not know how to understand this attack, how so many people could die so quickly, in such a desperate act of hatred. He did not want to flock to Spain to fight; how could he support his people from the safe confines of Paris, France?

He picked up the brush and readied himself to paint, and he began work on one of the most famous paintings of all time. It stood at an astounding twelve feet tall, more than three times the height of an average man; it also ran twenty-six feet long. He worked day and night, sometimes for hours at a time, relentlessly on *Guernica.*

Three weeks later, he put down the brush. Dora had supported him wholeheartedly throughout the project, and with a camera she took many photos of both Picasso painting it, and the painting itself.

Guernica is a painting that depicts suffering and pain. It is supposed to show the tragedy of the Guernica bombing, and it clearly conveys all of the emotions and destruction. When the painting was revealed to the public, it was very clear what it supposed to portray. People were very moved by all of the different events in the painting, the screaming people, the running animals, and the severed body parts. Everything in the painting seemed distorted and improper, which demonstrated how panicked everything was during the bombing.

While the war raged through 1937 and 1938, the year 1939 brought a whole new conflict. For months, Hitler had slowly been conquering more territories in Europe. Germany was ruled by a government referred to as the *Third Reich*, and Hitler's Third Reich was becoming supreme. He outlined and publicly professed his plans to conquer the nation of Poland, planning to "cleanse" the country of its Jewish citizens.

However, other countries were tired of Hitler's antics and his rising power. Once Hitler's armies moved toward Poland, the next world war finally erupted. The United States of America, England, France, and many other countries stood against the ruthless German Third Reich.

The French were terrified of a German bombing attack. What if the Germans bombed France like they had bombed Spain? What would happen if people died by the thousands, like they already had in other countries under attack from the Third Reich? Men like Picasso wondered what would happen if a museum was bombed—would all his art be simply destroyed in a matter of minutes? Museums across France shut down and locked up their art, determined to stand strong against Germany.

Picasso and his family gathered together and moved farther away into southern Spain; it was dangerous to be too close to Germany, in the case of an attack. However, as Picasso's family soon discovered, France could not hold out against the strong German forces. The Germans defeated the French in battle and, within days, German tanks were rolling down the streets of Paris, and the flags of the Third Reich were flying from buildings everywhere.

This news was absolutely devastating to Pablo Picasso. Paris! The city he had loved and live for was now under control by the enemy. What was he going to do? Should he stay in Spain, under the fascist control of Francisco Franco? Or should he return to Paris, under the iron fist of Adolf Hitler?

Proudly, with his chin held high in the air, and with his belongings with him, Pablo Picasso marched into the German-occupied city of Paris, France. Hitler's soldiers, called the Nazis (naht-zees), patrolled the streets and buildings everywhere. With him, Picasso took all of his painting materials. He might not fight World War II with a gun, but he would most certainly fight with his paintbrush and with his mind.

Under the Nazi regime in Paris, life was very difficult. The Nazis were at war with the Parisians, and the Parisians were technically their prisoners. The citizens were treated kindly. Laws were stricter. Food was scarce. People lived in fear of Hitler and his soldiers, even more so now that his soldiers were marching outside their homes.

The Nazis knew that Picasso was living in Paris, and they also knew that he was the one that painted *Guernica*. They knew that he did not like them and that he was interested in painting messages against them. Picasso would often hear loud banging on his door, only to find Nazi soldiers present to interrogate them. They accused him of being Jewish, and it was law that Jewish citizens were not equal to others. Already, the Third Reich had unjustly killed millions of Jewish people.

Picasso was not Jewish, however, and the Nazis could not arrest him. However, they had more than enough reason to imprison based on his opposition to their regime. If Picasso stood defiantly against the Third Reich, using his paintbrush as his sword, couldn't they just arrest him and put an end to his art? Well, some historians believe that officials in the Third Reich wanted to protect Picasso because they knew he was so famous. If they arrested, imprisoned, or even killed Picasso, it might make the German people angry, and that could be a threat to Hitler's power. So, Picasso was allowed to live safely under the German occupation of Paris—but the Nazis kept a particularly close eye on him and his work.

Much of Picasso's work showed the struggling poor. He wanted to give hope to the lower classes, showing them that people did recognize their troubles and that, one day, they might rise up against oppressors like Hitler. While Picasso fought the war from the safety of his house, battles were brewing in the streets of Paris.

French rebels launched an attack against the German soldiers in Paris, and they were joined by French and American soldiers marching into the city. Planes soared over Paris, American tanks plowed through the streets, and gunfire exploded around every corner. The Germans were no match for the combined forces of both France and the United States, and Germany soon surrendered Paris.

Picasso was thrilled when he realized that Paris was saved at last! He opened his doors and felt free, and the American and French soldiers were amazed to meet him. This was *the* Pablo Picasso, whose art had held out hope for many during the course of the war. He let soldiers take shelter and sleep in his house, and he was more than happy to show off his art to the men who had freed Paris.

World War II began in 1939, and it ended six years later in 1945. Throughout the war, people around the war had celebrated his art as standing against fascism and oppression, fighting both Franco's forces and Hitler's slowly-crumbling Third Reich.

Chapter 6: The End of Picasso's Life

Throughout World War II, and eight years after, Picasso spent his romantic life with Françoise. But, like all of his other relationships, it was not long before it fell apart. This time, though, it was Françoise who left him, and not the other way around. Picasso was shocked! Why would someone ever leave him?

But also like all of the other cases, Picasso quickly found another woman to fall in love with. Her name was Jacqueline, and they remained in France after they got married. Some people might think this is strange today, but Picasso married her when he was eighty years old! He loved her, and he thought they would make a great husband and wife. He did not care about his age, he just wanted to get married.

After World War II, Picasso had become absolutely famous. Buildings, cafes, museums, and schools across the world showed his art. His name was everywhere! Historians and scholars were always talking about him, his art, and the way it had impacted the Spanish Civil War and World War II.

Even at the old age of eighty, he painted day and night. He had painted well over one thousand paintings—he painted over one hundred of his wife Jacqueline alone—and many people revered him for this. As he got older, he painted more; mainly because his wisdom and experience had made him want to send out more messages. He wanted to paint and talk with people more, despite getting older.

He even managed to hit his ninetieth birthday. However, he had been suffering many health problems recently, and doctors were not sure how much longer he would last. On April 8th of 1973, Picasso lay sick and dying and bed, with a doctor by his side doing all he could to help. Right before Picasso died, he turned to the doctor and with his dying breaths, he spoke the words:

"Drink to me, drink to me health; you know I can't drink anymore."

The doctor reported these words to the public along with the news of his death, and the entire world began mourning. His wife Jacqueline and his children were devastated, along with all of his former girlfriends and wives. Around the world, tributes to Picasso and his art went up. Sales of his art increased exponentially, although of only a choice few; Picasso created, throughout his entire lifetime, fifty thousand work of art, each of them unique and well thought out.

Around the world, entire museums have been dedicated to preserving and showing off only Picasso's work, such as the Picasso Museum in Barcelona and the Picasso Museum in France.

Now that we have studied the life of the artist, we must understand his art. What *about* his art made it so influential? Where does his art rest within artistic culture and movements?

Chapter 7: The Eternal Art of Pablo Picasso

The world of art had been changing long before Picasso was born, and it continued to change throughout his lifetime. For a while, artists had been challenging existing "rules" of art, by experimenting and creating new ways of painting. Vincent van Gogh, for example, headed many efforts to paint differently as part of a *post-modernist movement.* We call the artists that tried to change the face of the artistic world *modernists.*

Pablo Picasso was very much a *modernist* artist. He took art into the new age through creative thinking and intriguing viewpoints. For example, some historians say that his painting "Les Demoiselles D'Avignon" is one of his top five famous painting of all time. The picture shows five women, one of them with an African tribal mask, is strange poses.

The details of the painting are by no means realistic. Unfortunately, this is what many people still wanted; they wanted to be able to live inside the painting through vivid details. For centuries, men before Picasso had been creating paintings that were lifelike (Leonardo da Vinci is still famous for his realistic and detailed paintings, such as the Mona Lisa).

Picasso was a little disappointed by the reaction to his painting. His style is very unique, and one must truly see it, and research to understand what it is like. Some of the time, his paintings are majorly blocky with clear defined lines that do not actually appear as such in real life.

Why did Picasso do this? If many people wanted him to paint realistic drawings, why did he not do that? It was not because he could not paint lifelike drawings. He most certainly could, and he *did*, of his many girlfriends.

Picasso thought differently than other people. He was one of the greatest artistic minds of the twentieth century, and he wanted to paint the women in a way different than people might automatically expect. His art was two-dimensional, which means it looked flat and as if it had no real depth; but was the point to create a lifelike drawing? What is the message of Les Demoiselles d'Avignon?.

Many art scholars have noted the odd way in which many of the women in the painting are twisting their bodies, exposing some parts while hiding others. What is the purpose of this? Some believe that Picasso is trying to show different parts of the female body in different places, in a truly creative way. Whatever he was trying to accomplish, he was certainly successful in attracting attention. While many scholars used to denounce the painting as an insult to the world of art, others have called it one of the greatest paintings of the twentieth century.

As Picasso continued to experiment with the paintbrush, especially his friend Braque, whose talent almost matched his, he began to realize that he was on the brink of inventing a new style of art altogether. Unlike most other paintings of the time, but like Les Demoiselles d'Avignon, Picasso liked to segment the things in his work into shapes like squares and circles. It was very different, and nobody had painted like this before!

This style quickly became known as *cubism*, and it was Picasso's signature trademark. The reaction to cubism at first was divided. It was so different that some people had trouble understanding his paintings and forming proper opinions.

When Picasso began painting pictures of his girlfriends and his wives, it was hugely important that they were not painted in cubist form. He instead painted them very lifelike and detailed, exactly as he saw them. His other work, however, was intended to serve as how he thought about things and how he looked out at the world. The loves of his life, however, were too beautiful not to be depicted exactly as they were. When you think about it, it is rather sweet!

Another one of Picasso's famous paintings is called "The Two Saltimbanques." Instantly, the moment you see the painting, you can tell that the two figures in it are truly said. This was painted during the time period of Picasso's life called the Blue Period, when he was very depressed. There is a heavy amount of blue in the painting, and it seems to embody all the sad and negative emotions that Picasso must have been enduring as he struggled through his early years.

"Saltimbanques" is the French word for "acrobats," which is extremely intriguing. The painting has nothing to do with acrobats, and from the very look of it, you would never know that the two people sadly sitting in the painting are acrobats. It is possible that Picasso was showing them not doing their job because they were sad, or possibly because they could never live up to expectations. If there is a painting that represents Picasso's Blue Period, it is this one.

When Pablo Picasso's good friend Carlos Casegemas committed suicide one year, during Picasso's Blue Period, Picasso was obviously very upset and disturbed. In order to rid himself of his sadness and frustration, he turned to the paintbrush and painted "The Old Guitarist." Most of the painting was created with varying shades of blue, depicting an elderly man hunched over his guitar. The picture is very sad because it seems as if the man can barely play, and is old and weak. This painting is also a strong representation of the Blue Period. "The Old Guitarist" is one of Picasso's paintings that did not involve the style of cubism.

One of Picasso's later paintings, called "Weeping Woman," depicts a woman's face in intense pain. It was not created during the Blue Period, but rather during the Spanish Civil War and two years before the outbreak of World War II. Many people think it is face of Dora Maar, one of Picasso's girlfriends. Allegedly, he would always call her the "weeping woman." Whether this is true or not remains to be seen. This was painted around the time of the Guernica bombing, so it is possible that it is just Picasso focusing all of his anger, frustration, and sadness into one painting. Nevertheless, even though the painting is unrealistic and strictly cubist, it is disturbing and touching. It truly has to be seen to be understood.

One of Picasso's final works is also one of his most famous. It is called *Self Portrait Facing Death*, and it is a self-portrait of Picasso. It can sometimes be hard to tell exactly who Picasso is trying to paint, especially because of his cubist style. It is terribly important to know that when Picasso painted this, he was near his death, around ninety years old. He knew that death was coming sooner or later, and he obviously needed to grapple with many issues that surrounds nearing death. How should be approach death? Should he be afraid? Should he succumb to fear, or should he stand brave against the end of his life?

Even though the self-portrait is painted in a cubist style, and even though it is not supposed to look realistic, a viewer can still see what Picasso thought of his approach to death. Scholars have been varying opinions on the painting. Picasso's eyes in the painting are unusually wide and open as if he is afraid, but other scholars think that he is looking death in the face with courage and valor. *Self-Portrait Facing Death*, however, was not the final self-portrait Picasso created.

There were others, many of them much more disturbing and senseless. Some of them were not cubist at all, but rather bland, consisting of black and white. This is what Picasso thought of himself as he faced death. It was not colorful and happy, like some of his other paintings. It was not blue and solemn, like the works of the Blue Period. The final self-portraits were disturbing and interestingly human. While they make not make sense at first, once the audience truly takes the time to think about each painting not literally, but figuratively, then they can mean so much more.

Picasso is blessed with a rare honor: his place in history is well-known and significant. Many artists have had a tremendously strong effect on culture and artistic movements, but Picasso's hand was very powerful in the politics of the Spanish Civil War and World War II. While many artists talk about life, Picasso used his art to inspire rebels and to give hope to those who thought that hope was lost.

The period of the Spanish Civil War and World War II is one of the most desperate and devastating times in world history, a time when a line was drawn in the sand between good and evil, when Picasso looked out his window and saw Nazi soldiers marching down the streets, when he heard of his own cities under attack, when he knew that his art was changing lives. Around the world, people looked at his art, and they saw a human struggle. They saw the devastation of *Guernica* and realized that the bombing was severe and terrible. It was a way of drawing attention to the rebels' cause and the destruction caused by the German army.

Like many artists around the world and throughout history, Picasso used connections with other artists to develop his skills. Braque, Casagemas, and others helped Picasso create the style of cubism. Cubism still remains as one of the most creative and lasting styles of the modernist art era.

Picasso absolutely revolutionized the world of art in the 1900s. While many people thought that artists needed to depict life as we saw it with our eyes, he knew that he could paint things as he saw them in his head. His thoughts and feelings were just as influential, perhaps more important than what he saw with his eyes. He knew that he would be able to convey more emotion, and deeper messages if his own feelings were able to bleed through the painting—and that is where cubism helped him.

Of all the artists of the twentieth century, Picasso stands out as being one of the most, if not *the* most, influential. His work against the Spanish fascists and the Nazi regime was critical is creating a culture that served to keep the hopes of rebels strong. Picasso's world was one of danger and death. He lived through bombings. He lived in a city under occupation by the world's most terrifying and feared army. And yet he lived to tell the story and even painted a few hours before his death at ninety-one years old.

There are many lessons to take away from Picasso, and not all of them have to do with artistic style. There is always hope, Picasso told us, whether you are fighting a war with a sword or a paintbrush. He did his part to help make the world a better place. His art is still observed and studied across the world. As long as there are wars, and as long as there is art in human society, Picasso will have a tremendously important place in our history.

Resources

Kelley, True. *Who Was Pablo Picasso?* New York: Grosset & Dunlap, 2009. Print.

https://geniusmothers.com/genius-mothers-of/famous-artists-writers-musicians/Maria-Picasso-Lopez/

http://web.org.uk/picasso/occupation.html

http://www.nytimes.com/learning/general/onthisday/big/0825.html

http://www.picasosgallery.com/pablo-picassos-most-famous-works.php

http://faculty.mdc.edu/nrodrigu/demoiselles/lesdemoiselles.htm

http://www.inminds.com/weeping-woman-picasso-1937.html

Vincent Van Gogh

Introduction

Vincent van Gogh was a spectacular artist, and one that has gone down as one of the most influential artists in the history of the world. But what made this man so special? What was it about his art that made him a celebrity? During the course of his lifetime, his art was extremely unpopular—so unpopular, in fact, that van Gogh infamously cut off his own ear. His influence only became known after he had died. Why was his art not famous during his life?

He died over one hundred years ago, but we still talk about his art today. There is something peculiar about his art, something that makes it different from the works of many other artists. Vincent van Gogh was a genius, from his birth to his death, and he is an incredibly interesting person to study. He had many personal problems that both drove and destroyed his art career. Van Gogh remains one of history's most famous artists, and his art is viewed by millions of people around the world.

Chapter 1: Early Life

Vincent van Gogh was born in the country of Holland, which is in northwestern Europe. His mother's name was Anna Cornelia Carbentus, and she was married to a reverend named Theodorus van Gogh. Theodorus was a reverend in the protestant church in Holland. Anna gave birth to her son on March 30th, 1853, in the town of Groot-Zundert. Neither of his parents knew that, one day, their son would grow up to be one the most hated, and the most loved, artists of all time.

Vincent grew up with three sisters and two brothers: Elisabeth, Wil, Anna, Theo, and Cor. While not much is known about Vincent van Gogh's childhood, we do know that he did not spend much time drawing or practicing to be an artist. However, Vincent's mother, Anna Cornelia Carbentus, enjoyed painting. It is thought that her love of art was passed down to her son, even if Vincent didn't like art right away. Anna liked painting watercolors, something that Vincent would experiment with down the road.

Watercolor painting involves paint that is partly made of water, giving the colors a clear and bright look. It is this bright look that defined many of Vincent van Gogh's most famous paintings. When studying van Gogh, it is crucial to understand why he started painting watercolors, or where he learned all of his information. We can assume that his mother played a strong role in his education as an artist!

As Vincent grew up, his parents noticed that he was a moody child. Vincent was often sad and angry, but no one knew entirely why at the time. He stayed in school until he was fifteen years old. When he was fifteen, his parents barely had enough money to keep the family going. It was difficult to feed six children and two parents. Vincent needed to quit school in order to find a job, something he did not really want to do. Even though he left school early, though, Vincent was still able to speak Dutch, English, German, and French fluently.

At first he was not sure where he wanted to get a job. Eventually, he worked with his Uncle Cornelis, who sold art for a living. His Uncle Cornelis worked with the Hague, which was a center for art in Holland. He worked there for six years until he was sent to London to work at a place called the Groupil Gallery.

Vincent had always wanted to visit London, and when he was there he became enamored with the city. He loved the city, he loved the people, and he loved British writers. He was a big fan of Charles Dickens, the author of famous classics like *Great Expectations*, *A Tale of Two Cities*, *Oliver Twist*, and the popular children's story, *A Christmas Carol*. While he was in England, he also enjoyed visiting many of the art galleries that the country had to offer. It is likely that he began to like art more and more, thinking about it more often. English art had a profound influence on van Gogh's life.

While in London, he also fell in love. There was a woman named Eugenie Loyer who caught his eye immediately, and Vincent was infatuated with her. He loved her so much, in fact, that he asked for her hand in marriage. Unfortunately, however, Eugenie said no.

Vincent could not handle the rejection; it nearly destroyed him. He had an emotional breakdown, and was not exactly sure what to do with his life. His love for her had been everything, and it was suddenly thrown away. He got rid of all of his books, except for one: the Bible. Vincent was raised in a religious household, especially since his father was a reverend for the protestant church. Vincent decided that he was going to spend his life serving God instead, ignoring his career in the world of art.

At the Groupil Gallery, the managers soon became acutely infuriated with Vincent, who was telling his customers not to waste their money on art, since he believed that art was not majorly important. The Groupil Gallery started losing business, and no one wanted to interact with the sad, angry van Gogh. The managers fired him, and Vincent van Gogh no longer had a job.

At this point, he was unsure of where to go, or what he wanted to do with religion. He decided to teach and preach the word of God, in a Methodist school and in a church. Vincent surrounded himself with many religious preachers and decided that he would like to become a minister, like his father. He was told that, in order to become a minister, he would need to go to Amsterdam, where the School of Theology was. *Theology* is the study of religion. The part *"theo"* means "god," and the part "*ology*" means "the study of." Put them together, and you get "the study of god."

But there was one thing that stopped Vincent from getting into the school. He studied hard for a whole year because each student needed to take multiple tests before getting into the school. One of these exams was on the Latin language—a language that Vincent was known for hating. He thought that cultured people around the world should no longer speak Latin and that only poor people should speak it. When the school discovered this, they were offended refused to allow Vincent in.

Dismayed yet again, Vincent decided to go the Church of Belgium. By this point, he was twenty-five years old and desperate to find solid work. He went into the coal mines of southern Belgium, a filthy, nasty place where workers never wanted to go. Vincent's job was to preach the word of God to the miners, and also to take care of them when they were sick. It was not the best job in the world, but Vincent did enjoy what he was doing. He enjoyed leading the miners' faith.

In the mines, he even began drawing pictures of the workers. The miners loved seeing their drawings, and Vincent was happy to draw them. He did not stay there for too long though. After two years, the committee that ran the Church of Belgium decided that they did not like the following that Vincent was getting in the mines. Too many people liked him, and they liked him so much that they even compared him and his preaching with that of Jesus Christ. Because of this, he was fired from the Church of Belgium.

Three times already, Vincent van Gogh felt like his life had been smashed to pieces. He felt like a failure at love, at education, and at preaching. What was left for him? He thought he might try to return to the art business—but this time, he would not be selling art. He would be creating it.

Vincent contacted his younger brother Theo, who was an art dealer like their uncle. Theo told Vincent that he would be able to give him enough money to support him for a while, until he found success as an artist. Vincent moved to Brussels, the capital of Belgium.

There was just one slight problem. Vincent van Gogh had no professional education whatsoever. Unlike many of history's other notable artists, he did not have daily practice. He did not show promise when he was a young child. He had never been an apprentice, he had never gone to art school, and people did not know him for his art. As a man in his twenties, he would have to start all over again.

Vincent began to teach himself art, reading many books on the subject and practicing on his own. He hoped that if he devoted himself wholly, he would find success. Eventually, his art became better and better, and he found that art made him happy. Despite this happiness, however, Vincent's love life caused trouble for him.

After his horrible rejection from Eugenie, Vincent fell in love with his cousin. At the time, it was not unusual for cousins to marry each other. Today, we think of that as wrong, but back then it happened quite often. His cousin rejected him, however, and Vincent was left alone once again. He fell in love with another woman named Clasina Maria Hoornik, who was not the greatest influence on Vincent.

Vincent van Gogh's family despised Clasina, and they told Vincent that they would stop sending him money unless he broke up with her. Reluctantly, Vincent agreed. His family's money was the only thing keeping him alive. If it were not for his brother Theo, Vincent's art career would never have started.

Angry, sad, and confused, Vincent fled Belgium to live in the Netherlands. He did not have a single home, but instead he moved around from place to place. During his time there, he painted the people, and he painted the beautiful landscapes. This was part of his practicing, something that would help his art later on.

Chapter 2: Van Gogh's Health Problems

Van Gogh is known for his popular art, but he is also known for many of the health issues that he suffered from. He had many *mental disabilities*, problems that involved his mind. Today, when some people think of an "artist," they think of someone who is moody and sad, usually thinking about life and all of the bad things in it. It is because of van Gogh that this image exists. He was the original brooding artist.

The first disability that van Gogh suffered from was something called *bipolar disorder*, which involves a person's emotions. *Bipolar disorder* makes someone feel tremendously excited and then majorly depressed, with no reason or justifiable change. Van Gogh would often paint remarkably quickly, without stopping, and then he would feel sad for several days. He would feel depressed, as if no one in the world loved him. His rejection from schools and tough love life only made his bipolar disorder worse.

Van Gogh was also an avid writer—too avid, though. He enjoyed writing so much that many doctors believed he had *hypergraphia*, which is when a person will continue to write without stopping. We have evidence of van Gogh's obsessive writing, and many websites have transcriptions of the hundreds of letters he wrote during the course of his life.

Van Gogh was prone to seizures, which means he got them a lot. A *seizure* is when someone with a certain condition loses control of their body, falling onto the ground, their muscles causing them to flail around. It is believed that the medicine he took for his seizures may also have caused him to see the color yellow everywhere. What is odd about this is that the color yellow is featured in a number of van Gogh paintings.

He also suffered from a couple conditions of poisoning. The first type is called *thujone poisoning,* which he got from drinking too much alcohol. Van Gogh thought that alcoholic beverages might help with his seizures and his depression, but he was wrong—it only made things worse. The chemical *thujone* also causes people to see objects in the color yellow, possibly another reason van Gogh loved the color.

Lead poisoning was the other type. He got this from using paint that had lead in it, and chewing pieces of dried paint. On many occasions, when van Gogh was feeling depressed, he even tried to drink the paint, because he thought it would kill him. Van Gogh's *bipolar disorder* made it extremely hard to live, and he often thought that death might be better. Luckily, he stayed alive for quite a while.

Van Gogh did much of his painting out in the sun. He wanted all of his paintings to feel real, so he would paint outside. In fact, van Gogh spent so much time outside that he often had *sunstroke*, which is when the heat would make his stomach feel bad. He felt nauseous and moody, and often got angry towards people.

Van Gogh's mental disabilities were a gargantuan problem in his life, and to cope with them took a lot of effort and willpower. Often they interrupted his painting and made him feel horrible about his work. His painting, however, sometimes acted as a cure for all of his problems.

Chapter 3: Becoming an Artist

Vincent van Gogh lived at a time when there many changes going on in the world. People were exploring art in new ways. During the 1800s, there was a popular artistic movement called *impressionism*. This was a technique that artists used to create paintings. By using lots of bright colors, the artists believed they that were giving a new feeling to their work. *Impressionist* artists needed to use bright colors, but also to paint the world around them very realistically.

Van Gogh, however, was not strictly an impressionist. He was part of a movement called *post-impressionism.* An artist who identified as *post-impressionist* wanted to do more than just paint the world around them. They wanted the paintings to convey feelings and emotion, and they wanted to experiment with the bright colors that they used. *Post-impressionism* is just like *impressionism,* except that there are not as many rules. Van Gogh liked having freedom in what he painted.

The art that van Gogh made helped him cope with his mental disabilities. After being rejected from preaching and his romantic life, art was the only thing he had. Many different people and things influenced his life as an artist.

For one, he was inspired by the impressionist movement. If he had never seen impressionist art, he would never have become a post-impressionist. He looked at art by famous artists like Henri de Toulouse-Lautrec and Pisarro, both popular among art-lovers at the time, and even art-lovers today.

To enhance his education, van Gogh even enjoyed looking at the works of Japanese artists. He found eastern culture to be magnificently interesting. He had always wanted to go to Japan, but his dream was never realized.

In the year 1888, when Vincent van Gogh was thirty-five years, he moved in the countryside in southern France. Despite the fact that his brother Theo was supporting him financially, he still received remarkably little money and was having trouble surviving. Paint, after all, was expensive. How was he supposed to stay healthy and still have enough money for paint?

This is when he began eating paint. He ate little else besides coffee and bread, and he began suffering physically as well as mentally. Yet he still continued to paint, even if he was in a supremely unhealthy state.

Theo was extremely worried about his brother Vincent's health. When he heard that Vincent was not looking too good, he called upon the artist Paul Gauguin. Paul was also a post-impressionist artist, who was good friends with Vincent van Gogh and his family. Theo asked Gauguin if he could check on Vincent and make sure that everything is okay.

Gauguin arrived at Vincent van Gogh's tiny yellow house hidden in the French countryside, and he stayed there for a while. However, his stay with Vincent was not happy. Vincent van Gogh was moody and often liked to argue and fight with Gauguin. One night, their arguments got particularly heated, and Gauguin stormed out of the house. Van Gogh followed him, and Gauguin saw that he had a razor in his hand. But van Gogh then disappeared.

That night, van Gogh cut off his own ear. This was a result of the emotional problems that he was suffering from, and his intense fights with Gauguin. Van Gogh felt like no one appreciated his art, and his lack of money upset him deeply. He hated not having food on the table to feed himself; he hated being in his thirties and not having a wife or children; he hated no one buying his art; and he hated that his brother had to send someone to keep an eye on him. On top of that, Vincent van Gogh's fluctuating moods did not help him at all.

So, drastically and unnecessarily, he took his own ear. The next morning, French police took him to a hospital called Hotel-Dieu hospital. Van Gogh ended up okay, but he did suffer from the loss of a lot of blood. The blood loss made him weak, and made him have even more seizures than normal. The doctors took care of Van Gogh for a few weeks, until he was finally released in the first week of 1889.

Like most of his life, Vincent van Gogh emerged from the hospital feeling alone and depressed, despite the moral and financial support of his brother Theo. Van Gogh thought that he would be able to find peace and happiness in painting, so he decided to return to art and the yellow house in which he lived. Until that happiness came, however, he knew that he would need to keep checking in at the hospital.

Vincent van Gogh lived in his home by day, and at night he would visit the hospital so that he could check in with the doctors. None of this helped, though. The people of the town had heard that van Gogh was a dangerous man. They wanted nothing to do with him. They wanted him gone, and gone for good.

The people were so angry that they all signed a petition, declaring that van Gogh should be moved to an *asylum*, a place where people with mental disabilities can receive help on a daily basis. When van Gogh heard about this, he was so ashamed that he decided to listen to the petition, and he admitted himself into the Saint-Paul-de-Mausole mental asylum.

Even in the asylum, however, he continued working on his art. Many of the paintings that he created in the asylum were shown to the public on art displays. This included "Starry Night," one of Vincent van Gogh's most famous works. Because of his bipolar disorder, he went on a painting frenzy, sometimes finishing one painting per day. This was an incredible feat, and yet van Gogh was never truly happy.

Despite the fact that his art was good, it was not as popular as he thought it should have been. He was constantly unhappy with his work, only believing that people everywhere hated it and hated him.

Chapter 4: The Potato Eaters

Today, people would pay millions of dollars for an original copy of one of Vincent van Gogh's paintings. It may be hard to believe, but he only sold a single painting during the course of his life. It sold for four hundred francs in 1890, which roughly equals seventy-eight dollars in today's American currency. His paintings did not become well known until after his death, which we will talk about later.

Many of Vincent van Gogh's works, even if people did not realize it at the time, were incredible, deep, and meaningful.

The Potato Eaters was one of van Gogh's first paintings and, posthumously, one of his most popular. *Posthumously* means after someone's death. Van Gogh finished painting The Potato Eaters in 1885, when he was still learning exactly how to paint. If you look at this painting and many of his later works, you can see that his skill really improved over time. But still, The Potato Eaters is a hugely impressive painting!

If you have not seen the painting, it shows five people eating potatoes around a dinner table. The painting is quite dark, which contrasts with many of van Gogh's later, brighter works. It is likely that he had not totally committed to post-impressionism yet.

What was van Gogh trying to do when he painted The Potato Eaters? Well, his artistic goal was to create a realistic work. He wanted his audience to feel like they were sitting at the table with the people in the picture, to hear their conversation, to see their illuminated faces. But when you look at the painting, it may be easy to overlook all of the details in the background. Vincent van Gogh paid special attention to the background, making sure that every inch of the painting was given equal focus. He believed that this would give it a realistic look, and he indeed achieved his goal.

What about the subject of the painting? What does it mean? It is clear to see that the five people in the painting are poor; they are most likely peasants, a common term for lower-class citizens in the 1800s and beyond. It is important to note that *potatoes* are commonly a sign for poverty. Since they grow in plenty and are harvested by many poor farmers, many peasants ate them. Besides the potatoes, though, the room in the painting is dark and the wood looks battered and slightly rotted.

No one in the painting has a happy expression on his or her face, and they look thin and bony. Their clothes are ragged and dirty; generally, they look like friends or family that has been working hard all day, and has come together at night to share food. Although there is no truly clear answer, Vincent van Gogh seems to be discussing the tough lives of the poor—something he would know very well since he struggled for money most of his life. It is possible that the somber and disappointed faces of the people in the painting also reflect many of his emotions.

Not only the people show sadness in the painting, though. The colors themselves are an indication of the painting's message. Most of the colors are dark, which sets the *tone*, or the feel, of the work. The only bright colors can be seen on the faces of the people, mixed in with shadows, showing their sharp and brooding features. Many of the colors in the painting are brown, gray, and green, colors that are associated with dirt and the earth, and also farming. This can represent all of the work that the peasants have been doing all day.

Many art scholars have called the painting *naturalist*, meaning that van Gogh painted things exactly as they should be painted. He did exaggerate anything within the painting, and all of the colors appear precisely as they normally would look inside the potato eaters' house. No light in the painting appears out of thin air; van Gogh does an excellent job with shading and recognizing that, in a house of peasants, the residents might not be able to afford the best light source.

So, now that you know what The Potato Eaters is all about, it's important to think about why it is important. Why should you care about this at all? This painting is a perfect example of how an author might reflect his or her feelings in her work— but not blatantly. This painting has a lot of meaning once you know more about Vincent van Gogh's life. When you think that he was poor, had barely any food, and was suffering from extreme sadness, you might feel some of this too, and even get a better understanding of what van Gogh went through.

Also, this painting most likely resonated with many of the peasants at the time, even if it did not become immediately popular. Not only does The Potato Eaters represent van Gogh's physical and mental state, it also gives a face to the troubles of many poor people at the time. This painting is a window into history, and a window into one of history's greatest and most intriguing minds.

Chapter 5: Vincent van Gogh and the Sunflowers

During the course of his lackluster artist career, Vincent van Gogh also experimented with a type of art called *still life*. Still life art is when the artist looks at an inanimate object and paints it just as it is, as someone walking by might see it. This was part of the *naturalist* movement, to paint things in their natural environment. Some of van Gogh's favorite things to paint were sunflowers. There are plenty examples of this.

The sunflower paintings demonstrate van Gogh's obsession with color yellow, as yellow is something that is often associated with sunflowers. Many of the paints have bright colors, but the sunflower paints can also show us something else about van Gogh, and something else about the nature of his art.

When we think of flowers, we usually think of life. We may even think of love. But what we do not usually think about is that flowers will always wilt and die eventually because they are living organisms. There are plenty of van Gogh paintings that show bright, lively flowers; but there are also plenty of van Gogh paintings that show dying flowers, using darker shades of yellow, and also colors such as dark orange, brown, and gray.

Looking at one single sunflower painting might not be that impressive, but when you look at all of them side-by-side, you can begin to see the contrasts and the comparisons between them. This bigger picture idea also relates to Vincent van Gogh and the mental problems he was enduring at the time. His moods switched from extremely excited and happy (*bright colors*) to sad and melancholy (*dark colors*). This is another reason that the sunflower paints are so extraordinary, despite the fact that they look so plain and simple at first.

So, what else makes them noteworthy? Why should students be paying attention to Vincent van Gogh's paintings of flowers? After his death, when people began to see the true beauty of his art, they realized what kinds of messages he was sending. Van Gogh's paintings were so simple, but they were able to convey such extreme emotions, felt by all humans and everyone who looks at them. Many people have tried to capture the emotion of van Gogh's paintings, but no one seems to succeed. Perhaps, because van Gogh felt so emotionally tied to his work, he was able to better put his feelings into his art.

The sunflowers are one good example of his still life, but Vincent van Gogh of course used other flowers in his work. He also enjoyed using irises and roses, some of his favorite flowers. Most of the time, he was unable to afford human models that he could paint, so finding flowers in the woods was an easy—and inexpensive—task. One of his best-known works, titled Irises, came from this.

He began work on Irises while in the mental asylum, after seeing irises there. Irises does not feature the swirly, warm style that is seen in many of Vincent van Gogh's paintings. It instead takes a rough, though realistic, approach, to a very beautiful scene—most likely something that not many art scholars had seen at the time, but that did not immediately come off as impressive.

Irises can currently be viewed in Los Angeles, California, at the Getty Center. It is one the most expensive paintings in the world! It was sold for fifty-four million dollars in the late eighties and might be even more expensive now.

Chapter 6: On A Dark and Starry Night

Before starting the painting *Starry Night,* Vincent van Gogh wrote that "At present I absolutely want to paint a starry sky. It often seems to me that night is still more richly coloured than the day; having hues of the most intense violets, blues and greens. If only you pay attention to it you will see that certain stars are lemon-yellow, others pink or a green, blue and forget-me-not brilliance. And without my expatiating on this theme it is obvious that putting little white dots on the blue-black is not enough to paint a starry sky."

Before diving into the subject of the painting, this quotation demonstrates that van Gogh is willing to see beyond the fact that night is dark. He sees the dark colors as beautiful, and the bright colors of the stars as something to marvel and wonder at.

Starry Night is most likely Vincent van Gogh's most popular painting, and arguably one of the most famous paintings in the history of the world. Not many paintings have been replicated and reproduced as many times as Starry Night has. Why is this? What makes Starry Night so captivating and special? It did not follow van Gogh's typical post-impressionist style, instead depicting the world as swirling and perhaps slightly disproportionate.

The painting Starry Night is mainly taken up by the swirling sky, which has different shades of blue and white. The moon and seven stars rest in the sky, casting light on the blue sky around them. The sky seems to have been painted with thick brush strokes that give the sky a sort of movement, almost like the waves of an ocean, a key to note for later. Below the sky sits a town with many houses and what appears to be a church steeple towering above everything else.

But many people notice the large, curvy, shadowy object that takes up a good portion of the painting on the left side—and no one is exactly sure what it is. Some people think it is a mountain, others think it is a castle, and some people think it is a bush or some form of vegetation.

The colors in Starry Night are contrasting, yet they go really well together. In the small town, many of the houses are dark. The darkness would usually bring up images of sadness and hate, but the audience does not get this image since some of the windows are illuminated. The town looks quiet and cozy and peaceful, something that van Gogh may have always wanted, but never actually achieved.

Once again, in Starry Night, you can see that van Gogh uses the color yellow. The color yellow is notable because it is the only vivid color in the dark sky. In fact, the color yellow is why the painting is called "Starry Night" in the first place; the stars need to have some importance!

It is clear that "light" is a truly crucial part of the painting. So what does "light" mean? Why should you focus on the "light" in Starry Night? Light is typically seen as something helpful. If you are walking on a dark path, the light from the moon and the stars can help you on your way. Van Gogh may have felt this way about a lot of things in life. While The Potato Eaters is a pessimistic—or a *negative*—painting, Starry Night appears hopeful. The colors are warm and beautiful, and you can feel hope when you look at it.

Many people think that the sky is another way of looking at the human mind—especially Vincent van Gogh's mind. Much of the time, he was confused. The swirling sky represents van Gogh's swirling and confused thoughts—and the light is the light at the end of the tunnel, the happiness that he can reach.

Scholars and professors who study art have noted that there are two main aspects of the painting: there is nature, and there are humans. While we do not physically see any humans, we know that they are there because there are houses and a church. While normally nature and humans are seen as two different things, everything in the painting seems to blend together and act as one. The painting is very even and harmonious, and easy to look at and grasp.

Despite the fact that humans and nature are living together, the humans appear to be asleep since there is no motion in the town; everything is still. The sky and the hills, however, were painted were curving brushstrokes. Van Gogh made it look like everything was in motion, like an ocean wave.

Starry Night may not be the most realistic painting; it is certainly not as realistic as The Potato Eaters. The sky and hills are not accurately painted, some of the colors are disjointed, and so on. So, strictly, Starry Night is not an *impressionist* painting, which wants to paint things truthfully and realistically. However, it is a *post-impressionist* painting because it focuses more on van Gogh's emotions and breaking the traditional rules of impressionism.

Chapter 7: A Self-Portrait of the Artist as a Young Man

During a three-year period, Vincent van Gogh created thirty self-portraits, all of them just a few years before he died. Many artists complete self-portraits, but what makes them so special? Why should we care what Vincent van Gogh's self-portraits look like? Well, when we examine what they truly mean to the artist, we get a deeper insight into their minds.

Artists are praised for their creative minds. So what happens when a creative mind thinks about itself? Van Gogh, as the original brooding artist, was a man of *introspection*, which means that he often thought about himself, his character, and his purpose in life. He used painting as a way to look upon himself, and to paint more than just his physical appearance. He thought that certain things within the painting could tell people what he was really like.

He only started doing self-portraits because he did not have enough money to pay for models to paint. So, who else better to paint than himself? It would save him money, plus he could probably learn a lot about himself. There are plenty of places where you find a full collection of Vincent van Gogh's self-portraits on the Internet, and you can measure the changes across the years, perhaps aligning his portraits with his life events.

It is fascinating to see the portraits of van Gogh before and after he severed his ear. While the self-portraits before the event make him look very realistic and proper, the one in which he has a bandage covering the right side of his face also makes his face look distorted, pale, and lifeless—perhaps representing how he felt at the time his depression was taking its toll on him.

Chapter 8: Van Gogh's Letters

Vincent van Gogh left more than just artwork behind. He is especially known for the letters that he left behind. Hundreds of them were recorded. Online, students can find the mostly complete correspondence that occurred between Vincent and his brother Theo.

It is one thing to study Vincent van Gogh's life, and it is quite another to read the loving words exchanged between him and his brother. It adds a new level of personality to Vincent and his distraught character. If you search for the letters on the Internet, you can see what Theo and Vincent were talking about—and there are literally hundreds of them, approximately nine hundred to be exact.

The letters are a good way to get inside the mind of van Gogh. What was he feeling at this point in his life? How was he communicating with Theo? Since Theo was the only reason that van Gogh was able to survive, giving him money and shelter when needed, the relationship between van Gogh and Theo is extremely important.

It's not just that there are so *many* letters that survived the test of time, but the fact that the letters themselves reveal so much about van Gogh's life. Hundreds of artists have left behind their letters to loved ones, but none of them tell historians so much as the ones of Vincent van Gogh do. Just by reading the letters, one can journey with the artist as he searches for his true calling as a child, grows up with many issues, and struggles to find comfort and support in his time as an artist.

There is an excellent example of the quality of van Gogh's letters. In one of them, he writes:

> "What am I in the eyes of most people — a nonentity, an eccentric, or an unpleasant person — somebody who has no position in society and will never have; in short, the lowest of the low. All right, then — even if that were absolutely true, then I should one day like to show by my work what such an eccentric, such a nobody, has in his heart. That is my ambition, based less on resentment than on love in spite of everything, based more on a feeling of serenity than on passion. Though I am often in the depths of misery, there is still calmness, pure harmony and music inside me. I see paintings or drawings in the poorest cottages, in the dirtiest corners. And my mind is driven towards these things with an irresistible momentum."

This quotation shows us a lot about van Gogh. He says that he is distraught and sad a lot of the time—but despite these rough feelings, he still manages to push through, find the happy things in life, and put them into his paintings. This would explain why, even though he suffered from so many dark thoughts, the subject of his art is bright. He still finds that he wants to show "love."

Chapter 9: How to Van Gogh Around the World

There is one thing that is incredibly important to understand about the life of Vincent van Gogh: the places he lived influenced his painting. *Location* played a huge part in his life, especially because he spent so much time moving from place to place and not having a real home. Many people say that this is also one of the reasons that he was so troubled all of the time. Whatever the reasons, though, van Gogh was a traveler, and if we want to understand his life, we have to understand where he had been.

Many people who visit Europe go on "Van Gogh Tours," in which they explore all of the places that Vincent van Gogh lived, in order to get a better idea of his life. If you wish to do this, it is a lot of fun (although it can get expensive), although this section will explore the importance of many of the settings in Vincent's life.

Vincent's Hometown

Unfortunately, the house where Vincent van Gogh was born is no longer standing. It was destroyed in 1903 and rebuilt. The new building, however, is the site of the Vincent van GoghHuis. This is a museum of all things van Gogh, and a great place for people to visit if they wish to learn more about the artist's childhood and general history.

Arles, France

In the city of Arles, France, there are many intriguing places about the life of artist Vincent van Gogh. If you ever visit the city, the Arles Visitor Center will have plenty of information of van Gogh's life and the cool places you can go. In Arles, you can visit places that were the inspiration for many of van Gogh's paintings, such as Starry Night Over the Rhone. It is extremely intriguing to see the scenery that van Gogh once saw so that we can understand his world better!

The Café van Gogh sits in Arles, France and remains a popular tourist attraction today. The building was not always called the Café van Gogh, however. Vincent used to paint here, and this building is the subject of his work, Café Terrace at night. If you look at pictures of the café now, and pictures of Vincent's famous painting, you can see the similarities immediately. Vincent painted this work on that spot, and so it is a popular area for tourists and art historians to flock to.

Many teachers, when telling their students about Vincent van Gogh, like to simulate a café in class, as a fun experiment in the type of food that Vincent might have been eating at the time (and it is delicious too!). In addition to this, many cafes that are van Gogh-themed have sprung up across the United States and some countries in Europe. Van Gogh has become a cultural icon in many places.

If you ever get the chance to visit Arles, France, you may also want to stop by the L'Espace Van Gogh, which is the new name of the hospital at which Vincent van Gogh cut off his own ear. Vincent even painted certain areas of the hospital's courtyard outside, so visitors are able to see exactly where van Gogh stood and painted, and what he saw through his own eyes.

Also in Arles, France is the Langlois Bridge, which was a popular place frequented by van Gogh. During the course of his life, van Gogh became obsessed with Japanese architecture and art. The western name for this at the time was *Japonisme*. When van Gogh was living, the world was not as *integrated* as it is today—there was not a lot of trade between different countries, like you see every day now. In 1856, Japan opened trade with many western European nations, so van Gogh saw an increase in Japanese artifacts.

Japonisme might be one of the reasons that van Gogh's later paintings were so bright. Much of Japanese art contained many bright and pure colors. Japanese art also involved depictions with strong outlines, one of the reasons that van Gogh's art was so popular and revolutionary. He also liked to have many contrasting colors in his paintings, very similar to the characteristics of Japanese artwork. Van Gogh painted a lovely picture of the Langlois Bridge, and you can compare his painting with the real thing!

In the town of *Auvers-sur-Oise*, there are a couple places that held extreme significance in the life of Vincent van Gogh. He painted an image of the garden of his doctor, Dr. Gachet, but the painting was created with a decidedly odd style. The brush strokes are more wavy and squiggly than usual, and many of the colors of darker, which could have represented van Gogh's state of mind while he painted the garden.

In addition to that, tourists can also visit *Le Maison de van Gogh. Maison* in French means "house." *Le Maison de van Gogh* actually used to be the inn of the Ravoux family, who helped him in his final days. Today, vistors are able to tour the inside and see the room where van Gogh died. The inn is still an operating restaurant, and it serves many of the traditional meals that van Gogh ate during his time there.

Finally, you can visit the grave of Vincent van Gogh. It sits at the top of a hill. Van Gogh was buried next to his brother, Theo. The two graves sit among a garden of vivid green plants with purple flowers sparkling throughout them. These plants and flowers were planted by the son of Dr. Gachet, in loving memory of the van Gogh brothers.

The Van Gogh Museum

In Amsterdam sits the Van Gogh Museum, where tourists will find dozens of paintings and artifacts from the life of Vincent van Gogh. The painting *The Potato Eaters* rests in this museum, along with plenty of sunflower paintings. The items on exhibit are divided into different times that they were painted in van Gogh's life, so that visitors are able to see how his paintings might have changed over time, and with his changing thoughts.

Most of these artifacts and paintings had belonged to Theodore van Gogh after Vincent died, but they have since been put into the museum so that the world can have access to van Gogh's mind and his life. In addition to paintings from van Gogh, other works stand in the museum, many of them piece of art created by impressionist and post-impressionist artists.

It is sad that all of this great art can only be held in a single place, but it is an exciting visit for anyone who can make the journey. The museum puts Vincent's landscape paintings, self-portraits, portraits, drawings, still lives, and other assorted works up for audiences to view and consider. The museum draws in hundreds of thousands of people each year, all wanting to get a better idea of van Gogh's life and his artwork.

Chapter 10: The Death of Van Gogh

While Vincent van Gogh was in the asylum, his first and only painting sold during his life. His painting, "The Red Vineyards" had been in the possession of his brother Theo, and it had sold for four hundred francs, the French form of money. Despite this victory in a sea of troubling debt and hopelessness, van Gogh's mental problems persisted. Theo desperately tried to find a doctor who tackle the problems that Vincent faced.

A man by the name of Dr. Paul Gachet was found, and he agreed to help Vincent. Van Gogh moved closer to Dr. Gachet, even though nothing good came of it. Instead of being helpful, the doctor and Vincent's family criticized him for the way in which he was spending, which destroyed Vincent. He thought that his family no longer supported his art career and that Theo would stop trying to get people to buy his art.

At this point in his life, he lived at an inn. He would often paint portraits of the innkeeper's thirteen year-old daughter, whose name was Adeline Ravoux. She spent much time with Vincent van Gogh, calling him "Monsieur Vincent" and enjoying his company. Adeline never saw that something might have been troubling van Gogh.

Theo knew that something was wrong with Vincent once again, and encouraged him to see Dr. Gachet. Vincent, however, refused to admit that anything was wrong. He said that all of his troubles and worries were far away. Even though Theo saw that Vincent was troubled in his letters, the innkeeper and his family saw nothing wrong. Each day, Vincent woke up at the same time, ate breakfast, and painted the morning away. He would eat lunch and dinner at the same time and he always spent the afternoon writing letters or spending time with the innkeeper's family. Nothing seemed out of the ordinary.

One morning, though, everything changed.

Vincent woke up normally, at the same time as always, and ate breakfast at the inn. He left to go paint. . . but he never came back for lunch. And he never came back for dinner. The innkeeper and his family began to worry. Why did Vincent not come back? He had had the same schedule for weeks, never breaking it.

At nine o'clock that night, Vincent returned to the inn. He was walking strangely—he was bent over and clutching his stomach. The innkeeper's husband said to Vincent, "Monsieur Vincent, we were anxious, we are happy to see you to return; have you had a problem?"

Vincent van Gogh only replied, "No, but I have. . ."

He never finished his sentence, so we will never know what he truly wanted to say. Some historians have tried to complete his sentence, but there is no way to know for sure. The Ravoux family knew that something was terribly wrong. After Vincent climbed upstairs and staggered into his room, the innkeeper went to his door to see if he could hear anything.

The innkeeper heard some moaning from the room, and decided to go in. What he saw shocked him. Vincent van Gogh lay on the bed, his hand closed on his chest. The innkeeper asked what was wrong, and Vincent lifted his hand and his shirt. There was a bullet hole in his chest. The innkeeper was horrified and asked what had happened.

Distraught, Vincent van Gogh had taken a pistol that morning, determined to finally kill himself. In July, He took a bullet to the chest—but as he failed in his art, so too did he fail in suicide. He bled profusely and fell unconscious, which is why he did not return for lunch and for dinner. At night, he woke up and realized that he was not dead but that he had survived his bullet. He returned to the inn, where he came across the innkeeper and his family.

When the innkeeper heard this story, he immediately called for Dr. Gachet, who came immediately. Dr. Gachet treated Vincent van Gogh's wounds, fearing that, even though van Gogh hadn't died yet, he would not have too much time left.

In the hospital, Vincent realized that maybe he did not want to die. He was indeed surrounded by family that was loving and willing to take care of him—perhaps he was wrong to try to take his own life. In one of his letters, he noted that "Close friends are truly life's treasures. Sometimes they know us better than we know ourselves. With gentle honesty, they are there to guide and support us, to share our laughter and our tears. Their presence reminds us that we are never really alone." This shows that van Gogh did truly care about the family and friends that surrounded him and that, despite all of his sadness and his anger, he knew that people did, in fact, care about him.

That night, as he lay in bed, he knew that he did not have much time left. Vincent turned to his brother Theo and asked to be taken home. Vincent van Gogh just wanted to go home. Unfortunately, however, this never happened.

A day after he shot himself, Vincent van Gogh died from loss of blood. He died at 1:30 in the morning.

Other people, however, say that there is a different story about van Gogh's death.

This story sets Vincent leaving the innkeeper's house at the normal time, like he did everyday. In the fields, as he was doing his early morning painting, he encountered two brothers, who were known to have been particularly mean to Vincent. One of the brothers was only sixteen years-old, but still they would play pranks on him and insult him and make him feel horrible about his art.

This story says that the two brothers tainted van Gogh's coffee with salt (which would give it an awful taste) and hid snakes in his paint box for him to find. Van Gogh was furious at the two boys, but he refused to punish them. One of the boys had a pistol with him, and he accidentally fired. The bullet shot off and went into van Gogh's chest.

Van Gogh, though, wanted to die, so he claimed that it was a suicide attempt so that the boys would not get in any trouble.

Which story do you believe? The first story is the one that most historians and scholars find the most credible, since the second story is mostly guesswork, and the facts do not seem to fully support it.

Vincent van Gogh's funeral was incredibly sad. All of his family and friends came, iand many people who did not know him, but knew of his artwork, including some other famous artists like Lauzet and Lucien Pisarro. Behind the closed coffin, all of his last paintings were arranged so that everyone could see his beautiful art. Flowers also surrounded the coffin, which was covered with a simple white sheet.

It is essential to remember that, since Vincent liked yellow flowers so much, yellow flowers could be seen everywhere at the funeral. His friends and family thought the van Gogh would have liked to have been buried with yellow flowers, especially since he thought the color was bright and hopeful.

At the foot of his coffin was also his easel, his painting stool, and all of his paintbrushes. It was a sad funeral, but it also a fitting farewell for one of the best-known and loved painters in the world. Despite the fact that Vincent van Gogh likely committed suicide and died from his injury, the funeral was still a time for remembrance. Everyone there looked at his paintings and marveled at their beauty and their thought. If people did not like Vincent van Gogh's paintings before, they started to now. They began to see the beauty and the humanity in his work—it was something like they had never seen before.

Chapter 11: The Legacy of the Artist

A student can learn about Vincent van Gogh's life from beginning to end, but that does not mean that he or she necessarily *understands* van Gogh and the implications that his work had on the world. Why exactly was he such a gigantic deal? Why, over one hundred and fifty years later, are we still studying his work? Why does a simple painting of a vase of sunflowers hold such significance to us? What separates van Gogh from the thousands of other artists who have been forgotten by popular history?

There is something about van Gogh's art that resonates within the human mind and soul. There is something special about it.

Vincent van Gogh did not just *paint* things. He poured all of his emotion and his thoughts into his work, and this is why it is so real to us. This is something that is rarely seen today, with so many artists painting just to get money. Van Gogh never started as an artist, and found that it was his true calling later in life. In a single decade, he completed dozens of works that are relished by students, scholars, and historians across the world.

Many artists have tried to recreate van Gogh's paintings, usually to no avail. It seems like van Gogh had a special talent that other people are rarely able to tap into. He certainly had a way with the paintbrush, creating beautiful drawings that combined emotion with excellent style.

Vincent van Gogh gave the world what is now known as the "artist persona." This is what people assume to be the typical personality of artists: moody and unsuccessful, yet willful and committed. He gave plenty of culture to the world of art and the set the stage for dozens of new celebrities to take the world stage and become famous with their artwork.

Van Gogh also gives hope to millions of people that suffer from mental disorders each year. It seems like mental disabilities are a growing problem as we become more aware of their presence in our society. They are here, and we must discover a way to deal with them. Van Gogh showed the world that, even though his mental disorders were sometimes too much for him to handle, he was still able to become a world-renowned poet, famous for more than a hundred years after his death. Depression, seizures, and bipolar disorder were no match for van Gogh; he took them on head-first, and succeeded.

During the final two months of his life, many of his paintings were darker in color than they had been previously. It is clear to see that Vincent van Gogh was not doing too well. He put so much of his energy and his emotion into his painting that viewers are able to know about the artist just by looking at his paintings.

It is important to understand that van Gogh's work was crucial in the development of the *Expressionist* movement. What was expressionism? It was similar to *impressionism* in a way, except that expressionism was focused on getting the artist to show emotion and spirit through their painting. Whether it was an expression of general feelings or an expression of the artist's identity is up to the creator.

During the time, many of the impressionists were too strictly confined within their own loose rules, and many of them were afraid to break the guidelines. They simply wanted to paint realistic paintings, and nothing more. Van Gogh took everything to a whole new level by fueling his paintings with intense emotion, emotions that he would share with his audience. One of the reasons that people continue to look at his art is because of the way they feel when they think about it.

Expressionist artists followed in Vincent van Gogh's steps, admiring his colors and the way in which he portrayed the world around him. His skill with the paintbrush is revered; very few artists have been able to pull off the same effect with the same emotion and feeling behind it.

Many famous artists were influenced by the work of Vincent van Gogh, including Pablo Picasso, Joan Miro, Willem de Kooning, and Francis Bacon. Without van Gogh's initial steps into the world of expressionism and experimentation, many artists would never have been as successful as they were. This especially includes Pablo Picasso, arguably one of the most famous artists to ever live. Picasso was involved in a type of are called *Cubism*—but before he committed to cubism, many of his paintings had elements of van Gogh's style sprinkled throughout them.

One thing is absolutely for sure—the world has been taken in the grips of van Gogh-mania. Throughout the world, people are obsessed with Vincent van Gogh and his artwork, hanging his paintings in houses and office buildings, putting the designs on bags and other souvenir items, and converting restaurants into places that are specifically designed to be van Gogh-themed. It is extremely rare for any other artist to be idolized in this way. So what's so different about van Gogh? Why doesn't da Vinci have his own chain of restaurants?

People seem to connect well with Vincent van Gogh, probably because he went through so many issues, just like many of us do. He understood the poor, and he understood rejection and failure. But despite the many times that he found himself faced with the roughest of troubles, he was always able to pull through and create beautiful works of art. Obviously, in the end, van Gogh was defeated by his debilitating mental illnesses, but he did not go down without a fight.

In one of his letters, Vincent van Gogh wrote "Love is eternal - - the aspect may change, but not the essence. There is the same difference in a person before and after he is in love as there is in an unlighted lamp and one that is burning. The lamp was there and was a good lamp, but now it is shedding light too, and that is its real function. And love makes one calmer about many things, and that way, one is more fit for one's work."

As always, Vincent used light as a symbol for hope. When one looks at his paintings, it is impossible to miss the fact that van Gogh was particularly hopeful. Many of his works are beautiful and bright. To him, this meant that he was searching for a way out of his depression; he only wanted happiness. To us, this means that we can appreciate how he felt because we have felt it at one time ourselves. The art of Vincent van Gogh is the art of the human mind and the human experience.

As long as there are humans in the world, we will be studying Vincent van Gogh, his paintings, and his letters. They tell the story of a frail human who sought happiness and peace from one of the only thing that separates humans from other animals: art. Vincent van Gogh is a tribute to humans everywhere, and his paintings will continue to be celebrated and revered.

Resources

http://www.biography.com/people/vincent-van-gogh-9515695

http://www.vangoghgallery.com/misc/overview.html

http://www.ibiblio.org/wm/paint/glo/impressionism/

http://www.vangoghgallery.com/influences/post-impressionists.html

http://www.vangoghgallery.com/painting/potatoindex.html

http://designercityline.wordpress.com/2010/03/15/writing-analysis-of-the-potato-eaters-by-van-gogh/

http://www.artble.com/artists/vincent_van_gogh/paintings/starry_night/more_information/analysis

http://www.vggallery.com/visitors/002.htm

http://usatoday30.usatoday.com/travel/destinations/2009-10-11-van-gogh-letters-amsterdam_n.htm

http://www.vangoghmuseum.nl/vgm/index.jsp?page=425&lang=en&section=sectie_museum

http://www.artyfactory.com/art_appreciation/art_movements/expressionism.htm

CPSIA information can be obtained
at www.ICGtesting.com
Printed in the USA
LVHW05s0750280918
591585LV00013BA/1077/P

9 781495 303333